The Big Book of
Humorous
Training Games

Doni Tamblyn

Sharyn Weiss

McGraw-Hill

New York   San Francisco   Washington, D.C.   Auckland   Bogotá
Caracas   Lisbon   London   Madrid   Mexico City   Milan
Montreal   New Delhi   San Juan   Singapore
Sydney   Tokyo   Toronto

The Big Book of Humorous Training Games
Games to bring humour, fun and creativity into any group situation

Doni Tamblyn and Sharyn Weiss

ISBN 13: 978-0-07-711507-4
ISBN 10: 0-07-711507-4

 **Professional**

Published by:
McGraw-Hill Publishing Company
Shoppenhangers Road, Maidenhead, Berkshire, England, SL6 2QL
Telephone: 44 (0) 1628 502500
Fax: 44 (0) 1628 770224
Website: www.mcgraw-hill.co.uk

British Library Cataloguing in Publication Data
A catalogue record of this book is available from the British Library.

McGraw-Hill books are available at special quantity discounts. Please contact
the corporate sales executive.

Reprinted 2007

The *McGraw·Hill* Companies

Contents

Find the Perfect Game for Your Topic   *ix*

Introduction: How to Use This Book   *xiii*

Chapter 1. Five Games to Make You a Naturally Funny Trainer   *1*

Game 1—What's Inside?   *3*

Game 2—"Poets, Don't We Know It!"   *6*

Game 3—Psychic Buddies   *9*

Game 4—The Forgetful Storyteller   *13*

Game 5—Bomb with Aplomb   *17*

Chapter 2. Five Games to Enhance Creative Thinking and Problem-Solving Skills   *21*

Game 1—Numbers Don't Lie   *23*

Game 2—Brain Fry   *27*

Game 3—Free Association   *30*

Game 4—Random Access   *34*

Game 5—Playbook   *38*

Chapter 3. Five Games to Create Intrinsically Motivating Managers   *43*

Game 1—Alpha Leaders   *45*

Game 2—Look, Ma, No Hands   *50*

Game 3—Confucius Says   *56*

Game 4—Madison Avenue Talent Agents   *60*

Game 5—The Hiring Game   *65*

Chapter 4. **Five Games to Construct Creative, Cooperative Teams**   **73**

Game 1—Group-Mind Story   75

Game 2—Kommunication Krazy Kwilt   79

Game 3—Pushy Partners   83

Game 4—One Little Word   86

Game 5—Clash of the Titans   89

Chapter 5. **Five Games to Help People Deal with Change**   **95**

Game 1—Goodies Auction   97

Game 2—The Fear Drag   114

Game 3—Wedding Guests   118

Game 4—May the Forces Be with You   125

Game 5—Squishy Toy Company   131

Chapter 6. **Five Games to Develop Relaxed, Engaging Speakers**   **139**

Game 1—Phrase Ball   141

Game 2—Gibberish Experts   144

Game 3—Pillars   149

Game 4—Who Cares?   154

Game 5—Elementary, My Dear Watsons   158

Chapter 7. **Five Games to Increase Emotional Intelligence**   **165**

Game 1—Emotional Contagion   167

Game 2—As the Company Turns   172

Game 3—Selling Snow Plows to Hawaiians   180

Game 4—Take Me ... Please   184

Game 5—The Ideal Workplace   189

Chapter 8. Five Games to Reduce Workplace Negativity **193**

Game 1—Who Started It?   195
Game 2—Name That Norm!   198
Game 3—A Perfect World   204
Game 4—Alphabet Soup   207
Game 5—Take the Pledge!   211

Chapter 9. Five Games to Help Employees Deal with Difficult People **215**

Game 1—Calm Down You But   217
Game 2—Mirror, Mirror   222
Game 3—Name That Quadrant!   228
Game 4—Pickin' Up Those Vibes   234
Game 5—Scripts   241

Chapter 10. Five Games to Take the Fear Out of Assertiveness **253**

Game 1—Sculptures   255
Game 2—Stuck in the Middle with You   260
Game 3—Animal Kingdom   264
Game 4—Shoot-Out at the O.K. Corral   267
Game 5—Bizarro Expert   274

Find the Perfect Game for Your Topic

GAME	Page Number	ASSERTIVENESS	DEALING WITH CHANGE	COMMUNICATION SKILLS	CUSTOMER SERVICE	CREATIVE PROBLEM SOLVING	CONFLICT AND NEGOTIATION	DEALING WITH DIFFICULT PEOPLE	EMOTIONAL INTELLIGENCE	FACILITATION SKILLS	HOW TO BE A NATURALLY FUNNY TRAINER	ICEBREAKER	LEADERSHIP SKILLS	MANAGEMENT SKILLS	REDUCING WORKPLACE NEGATIVITY	PERSONALITY INVENTORY	DEALING WITH STRESS	SPEAKING SKILLS	TEAM BUILDING	VALUES
WHAT'S INSIDE?	3		X			X					X							X	X	
"POETS, DON'T WE KNOW IT?"	6					X					X	X		X	X			X	X	
PSYCHIC BUDDIES	9		X			X	X	X	X		X	X		X	X			X	X	
THE FORGETFUL STORYTELLER	13					X	X	X			X			X	X			X		X
BOMB WITH APLOMB	17	X			X	X				X				X	X					
NUMBERS DON'T LIE	23	X				X					X							X		
BRAIN FRY	27					X														
FREE ASSOCIATION	30					X														
RANDOM ACCESS	34		X			X													X	
PLAYBOOK	38				X	X					X							X	X	
ALPHA LEADERS	45						X	X						X		X				X
LOOK, MA, NO HANDS	50			X			X							X						
CONFUCIUS SAYS	56	X	X	X	X	X	X	X	X	X	X	X	X	X	X	X	X	X	X	X
MADISON AVENUE TALENT AGENTS	60													X					X	
THE HIRING GAME	65								X					X						
GROUP-MIND STORY	75		X			X													X	
KOMMUNICATION KRAZY KWILT	79								X			X		X					X	

GAME	Page Number	ASSERTIVENESS	DEALING WITH CHANGE	COMMUNICATION SKILLS	CUSTOMER SERVICE	CREATIVE PROBLEM SOLVING	CONFLICT AND NEGOTIATION	DEALING WITH DIFFICULT PEOPLE	EMOTIONAL INTELLIGENCE	FACILITATION SKILLS	HOW TO BE A NATURALLY FUNNY TRAINER	ICEBREAKER	LEADERSHIP SKILLS	MANAGEMENT SKILLS	REDUCING WORKPLACE NEGATIVITY	PERSONALITY INVENTORY	DEALING WITH STRESS	SPEAKING SKILLS	TEAM BUILDING	VALUES
PUSHY PARTNERS	83			X	X		X	X							X				X	
ONE LITTLE WORD	86			X			X								X				X	
CLASH OF THE TITANS	89									X			X	X			X		X	X
GOODIES AUCTION	97	X	X				X													X
THE FEAR DRAG	114	X	X						X						X					
WEDDING GUESTS	118		X						X						X		X			
MAY THE FORCES BE WITH YOU	125		X				X		X					X	X					
SQUISHY TOY COMPANY	131		X			X								X	X		X			
PHRASE BALL	141									X	X							X		
GIBBERISH EXPERTS	144									X	X							X		
PILLARS	149					X					X							X	X	
WHO CARES?	154										X							X		
ELEMENTARY, MY DEAR WATSONS	158					X					X							X		
EMOTIONAL CONTAGION	167			X					X						X		X		X	
AS THE COMPANY TURNS	172			X				X	X										X	
SELLING SNOW PLOWS TO HAWAIIANS	180			X					X						X					X
TAKE ME ... PLEASE	184			X					X					X	X				X	
THE IDEAL WORKPLACE	189						X	X	X				X		X	X			X	X

GAME	Page Number	ASSERTIVENESS	DEALING WITH CHANGE	COMMUNICATION SKILLS	CUSTOMER SERVICE	CREATIVE PROBLEM SOLVING	CONFLICT AND NEGOTIATION	DEALING WITH DIFFICULT PEOPLE	EMOTIONAL INTELLIGENCE	FACILITATION SKILLS	HOW TO BE A NATURALLY FUNNY TRAINER	ICEBREAKER	LEADERSHIP SKILLS	MANAGEMENT SKILLS	REDUCING WORKPLACE NEGATIVITY	PERSONALITY INVENTORY	DEALING WITH STRESS	SPEAKING SKILLS	TEAM BUILDING	VALUES
WHO STARTED IT?	195								X			X			X				X	
NAME THAT NORM!	198														X					
A PERFECT WORLD	204														X					
ALPHABET SOUP	207					X									X				X	
TAKE THE PLEDGE!	211														X					
CALM DOWN YOU BUT	217			X	X		X	X	X					X	X			X		
MIRROR, MIRROR	222	X		X	X		X	X		X			X	X				X		
NAME THAT QUADRANT!	228			X			X	X					X	X			X			
PICKIN' UP THOSE VIBES	234	X		X	X			X	X										X	
SCRIPTS	241	X		X	X		X	X											X	
SCULPTURES	255	X		X			X													
STUCK IN THE MIDDLE WITH YOU	260	X						X												
ANIMAL KINGDOM	264	X		X			X	X							X				X	
SHOOT-OUT AT THE O.K. CORRAL	267	X		X			X	X											X	
BIZARRO EXPERT	274	X						X							X					

Introduction: How to Use This Book

You can use humor in training. Naturally. Expertly. Gracefully. Appropriately. And best of all, to enhance learning and retention.

Most trainers already know that humor—used right—can bring any training topic alive. Unfortunately, many trainers believe they are not naturally funny people. Humor is a gift, they think. If you weren't funny back in Junior High, then you certainly won't be an amusing adult.

The fact is, humor *is* a gift—and *everybody* is born with it. Humor is measured not by people's ability to tell jokes or use novelty store items, but by their ability to play. And anybody who has ever been a child is an expert at playing. We assume that despite your current role as a teaching professional, you are, in fact, a former child. That means you already know how to use humor in learning games. You may just be a little rusty.

The Big Book of Humorous Training Games capitalizes on the joy of playful learning with 50 original humorous training games. Throughout the book we also offer tips on how to present the games in a way that will help your learners learn better and more enjoyably. Feel free to adapt all ideas in this book to fit your own style and the logistics of your training session. For instance, each game comes with a suggested "Funny Introduction." You do *not* need to memorize, or even use, the introduction. It is merely a suggested way to transition into the learning material while signaling to your learners that it will be entertaining as well as useful. We also show how to use humor to get willing volunteers for activities. We offer "ad lib" response to predictable learner witticisms.

We suggest debriefing questions to help deepen your learners' understanding of the material. Notice that most games in this book can also be used to introduce or highlight other topics by shifting the focus of the debriefing. (You will see this list of alternative topics at the end of each game, and also in the matrix at the beginning of this book.)

How You—Yes, *You*—Can Be a Humorous Trainer

We have two goals in writing *The Big Book of Humorous Training Games*. The first is to offer you a collection of playful exercises to build important business skills with your learners. The second is to help you as a teaching professional heighten your level of confidence in your innate ability to use humor as a training tool. That's why we suggest you start with Chapter 1, "Five Games to Make You a Naturally Funny Trainer."

The games in Chapter 1 illustrate the principles of what we call "natural" (as opposed to comedy club) humor. These principles are:

1. Don't Try to Be Funny—Just Try to Have Fun
2. Cut Yourself (and Others) a Little Gosh-Darned Slack
3. Focus Outward
4. Make Positive Choices
5. Acknowledge the Bomb

We will briefly describe these principles here, and offer practical suggestions as to how you might apply them in your own work.

Don't Try to Be Funny—Just Try to Have Fun

Trainers who try to *be funny* often do not care about their learners. They use their workshops as opportunities to get attention and approval for themselves. But being a trainer is different from performing in a comedy club. You are not in the classroom to entertain—you are there to teach.

Trainers who like to *have fun*, on the other hand, simply see delightful things about the world in general, including their learners. They appreciate anything that inspires laughter; it doesn't have to come from them. Essentially, they use humor to keep from taking themselves too seriously, to lighten things up in general. Their gift lies not in always being ready with a *joke*, but in usually being ready with a *laugh*. This is the kind of trainer you want to be: someone who enjoys your learners and the learning process.

Cut Yourself (and Others) a Little Gosh-Darned Slack

Naturally humorous trainers don't expect to be perfect. They allow for mistakes. They are playful as opposed to judgmental. As such, they often find that (1) they have more ideas to choose from and (2) those ideas are more far-reaching, more innovative, and more "outside the box"—better solutions, in short, to the problem at hand.

Let's face it: Inevitably you will lead a training session when the electricity goes out, or a work crew pounds on the training room walls, or half the learners get lost on the way to your workshop and scurry in, forty minutes late.

Welcome these situations as opportunities to develop your sense of humor and, concurrently, your creative thinking skills! By modeling an ability to laugh and deal with the situation at hand, you will create a tolerant, learner-friendly environment, in which all participants will feel respected, trusted, and empowered. It will also be an environment in which good thinking can take place.

Focus Outward

Virtually every professional stand-up comic will agree: Their biggest audience laughs usually come not from their best jokes, but from *spontaneous exchanges between themselves and individual audience members.*

This is important information for a stand-up trainer. Why? Because it means you don't have to be a comedic genius to inspire great laughs! The fact is that the best opportunities for humor happen in highly interactive settings. Learners know something really exciting: that anything might happen in this environment. More importantly, they know that *anyone can be part of the show!* This creates a kind of "tingle" that invites free and easy laughter. You can easily inspire this tingle by generously sharing the spotlight with your learners. Here are some ways to do this:

- Respond genuinely to their comments rather than just giving a noncommittal, "Mm-hm" or "I see" or a facetious "Yeah, great."
- Invite other learners to answer the questions of their colleagues.
- Make discussion groups a big part of your learning format. (This greatly improves long-term memory, by the way.)
- Give outlines of subsections of the curriculum to learner teams, and let them teach these to the rest of the class.
- Make greater use of your learners as "guest experts." Invite them to address the class when they happen to have specialized knowledge about a subject you are covering, or when they've had an experience that illustrates something the group is learning.
- *Above all, design programs that are not too information-dense!* How does this technique use the "Focus Outward" principle, you ask? All kinds of studies exist to show that dense curriculums look good only on paper. One reason is that they do not allow enough time

for learners to *ask questions*, an act that is vital to long-term learning. Designing your programs with lots of Q&A time is an especially important way to "share the spotlight."

- And the single best way to Focus Outward: *Be your learners' biggest fan!* Exhibit as much, if not more, interest in their contributions as in your own. Here are some ways to do this:

  Always laugh at their humor (as long as it is not inappropriate; see below).

  Even better, *repeat* their witticisms to the class at large to make sure everyone heard (this one pays huge dividends—believe us!).

  Make a point of mentioning a learner who had a useful question or comment at break.

  Do anything else you can think of to transfer ownership of the learning process to its rightful owners—your learners.

Make Positive Choices

Many studies have shown that both cognitive and creative thinking improve dramatically when mental imagery and the related emotions are positive. So it is important that you communicate in ways that "feel" positive to your learners. This involves getting into a habitually positive mindset, which can show up in:

- Using positive verbiage: "This will help" instead of "This will eliminate problems."
- Humorous acknowledgments of your own bloopers: "Please—hold your applause. There's more where that came from." (For more on this, see "Acknowledge the Bomb" below.)
- Most importantly, a *habitual stance of acceptance*: "Tell me more about your idea" instead of "I'm not sure that will work."

All these kinds of behaviors can help transform your learning environment into one that enhances brain processes. And isn't that the kind of environment you want?

Acknowledge the Bomb

Professional comedians (and naturally funny trainers) accept one inevitable fact: *Sooner or later, everyone bombs.*

It's time for you to know and accept this too. The good news is that if you handle a bomb honestly and elegantly, you can (1) deepen your learner's respect for you and (2) model professional risk taking for your learners. If an activity does not go as expected or hoped, we suggest an amazingly simple and yet devilishly clever technique: Acknowledge it immediately to the group. Then, in a stupendous act of bravado, thank your learners for demonstrating that the idea didn't work. (And then, because you are a gifted trainer, use the situation as a stepping stone to learn more about your learners' needs, motives, fears, and styles.)

When you can do this without fail, we guarantee that, master joke teller or not, you will be seen as someone with a *great* sense of humor! And now for a subject we would be remiss in ignoring ...

Inappropriate Humor

Much has been written about what constitutes inappropriate humor in the workplace. We will boil it down to one easy-to-remember rule:

You may only make derogatory jokes about *yourself* or a group *you* belong to.

It's really that easy. Examples:

- Sharyn and Doni can safely make jokes about women, but not about men: "If a man speaks in the forest, and there's no woman to hear him, is he still wrong?"
- We are safer making jokes about trainers than engineers: "How many curriculum designers does it take to effect a kidnapping? Six—one to kidnap the victim, and five to write the ransom note."
- If *you* mispronounce a word, it's fine to say, "Hm ... oral dyslexia."
- If *you* lose your train of thought, you are allowed to say, "I seem to be going through mental pause."

A *little* self-effacing humor can actually create a bond between you and your listeners. We recommend that you don't engage in too much of it—you don't want your learners suggesting you seek therapy—but do feel free to engage in it occasionally.

Remember: You must never disparage or poke fun at any of your learners. We don't care how dumb the question or comment may seem, insulting them (or people like them) will create distance. If you embarrass one of your learners, none of the others will trust you. You can take that to the bank.

And now you're on your way! Time to take a few risks, try some new things. Stretch yourself. Break a leg, as show people say. But most importantly ... Time to have fun!

Five Games to Make You a Naturally Funny Trainer

This chapter describes games that will help you to stretch your "funny" muscle. We encourage you to play these games with a partner before you train a group of new trainers on these skills. The games are organized sequentially. We suggest you teach or practice these games in the order they appear.

GAME 1—WHAT'S INSIDE?

THE POINT OF THIS GAME

Naturally funny trainers **do not focus on being funny**. They focus on ways to make training more fun. The world is a veritable hotbed of humor. Everything you need is already here; you just have to relax to open the conduit between the world and you. This game helps your learners relax their creative muscles, thereby allowing more funny moments to happen naturally.

TIME NEEDED

10 minutes

MATERIALS NEEDED

Only your imagination

A SUGGESTED FUNNY INTRODUCTION

[Hold up your hands as if carrying a cardboard box approximately 2′ × 2′ × 2′ in size.]

"I am holding in my hands a box that doesn't exist. Can everyone see it? [Look serious; your learners will undoubtedly nod. Ask one:] How big is it? [No matter what the answer, say:] That's *right*. Everyone agrees? [Comedy note: If your learner said the box was either very large or very small, adjust yourself physically to look like someone holding a box of that size.] This is a magic box. And in a moment, you will be surprised to find that half of you have just such a box under your chair. Let's see which of you do." [Mime tossing your own box away, and begin the game.]

HOW TO PLAY THIS GAME

1. Divide your learners into pairs. The person in each pair who is wearing the biggest watch will be Person A. Ask all Persons A to bring out their "boxes" from under their chairs. Then explain the game.

2. Person A will hold the "box" out to Person B and then say, "Hello, partner, tell me what *funny* things are in this box?"

3. Person B must immediately reach in, pull out an imaginary object, and name it. That's it. There are no wrong answers; there's just one hitch: *It must be funny.* Maybe it's a pink chicken; maybe a written plan for taking over the world with oven forks; maybe a hairy, nude CEO lolling in a hot tub (this is, after all, a *magic* box—dimensions are meaningless). Person B must keep drawing funny things out of the box one after the other, as *quickly as possible,* until his or her brain fries. This will probably happen quickly.* When it does, Person B should stop at once.

4. Now Person B gets to take the box out of Person A's hands and sweetly say, "Your turn." And so it is. Person A now pulls witty, hilarious things out of the box, as quickly as possible, till his or her own brain fries.

5. Both partners take a nice, refreshing drink of water.

6. Person A again holds out the box to the partner but this time says: "Hello partner, what *banal, boring, and unfunny things* are in this box? Repeat the process with each partner naming items until their brains fry (usually 1 to 3 minutes).

DEBRIEFING QUESTIONS

• What differences did you notice between the first time, when you were trying to be funny, and the second round, when you

*By the way, the colorful term "brain fry" comes from the equally colorful world of theatre improvisation. It describes the moment when your brain seizes up like an unoiled engine, rendering you suddenly unable to remember your own name. It is a disconcerting phenomenon, but studies show it does no lasting neural damage. In fact, it's good for you! For a game designed to deliberately induce brain fry, see Chapter 2.

were trying to be banal and unfunny? Which round was easier to do? When did you have most of your ideas?

KEY POINT: During the second round, when you were trying not to be funny, did one or two funny ideas still manage to slip through? (*Note:* This will have happened with at least some or your learners. Invite them to share these ideas with the class, and lead the laughter. Then remind learners that if unplanned funny stuff can pop out in a 1- to 2-minute exercise, it will certainly show up in a training schedule!)

- What were you thinking during the first round when the pressure was on to be funny?

- What is likely to happen if you stand in front of a group with this same internal pressure to be funny?

OTHER TOPICS THIS GAME TEACHES

- Creative Problem Solving
- Speaking Skills
- Dealing with Change (e.g., dealing more *creatively* with change. Replace "Don't be funny" with "Don't be original.")
- Team Building (for group brainstorming sessions; again, the mandate is "Don't be original")

GAME 2—"POETS, DON'T WE KNOW IT!"

THE POINT OF THIS GAME

Naturally humorous people are **spontaneous and quick on the uptake**. At least, they appear to be. Spontaneity, however, is a skill developed (or actually *relearned*, since we were all spontaneous as children) over time. Trainers who develop a reputation for being funny have successfully lived through those inevitable moments when they were *not* funny—could not think of a single response—and forged ahead only because they constantly saw possibilities in the unexpected.

This game will help your learners recall their natural spontaneity and become more comfortable about "coming up blank."

TIME NEEDED

10 minutes

MATERIALS NEEDED

Flip chart listing the four kinds of rhyme (optional)

A SUGGESTED FUNNY INTRODUCTION

"Only if you're meditating do you *want* to have an empty mind. If you're in front of a group, having an empty mind soon leads to having a sinking feeling. It's time to confront that fear. It's time to embrace fallibility. It's time, in short, to throw yourself into a game in which you are *guaranteed* to "come up empty," and have a blast doing so."

HOW TO PLAY THIS GAME

1. Post on a flip chart or describe to your learners the four kinds of rhyme in poetry:
   - **The 'perfect' rhyme:** *Fine* rhymes with *line* (as in "I want to be a poet fine, and so I rhyme with every line").

- **The 'good enough' rhyme:** *Fine* also rhymes with *find*. ("I want to be a poet fine, and so I use what rhymes I find.")
- **The 'coasting' rhyme:** *Fine,* amazingly enough, also rhymes with itself. ("I want to be a poet fine; behold, I *am* a poet fine!")
- **The most vital, all-important, 'So sue me' rhyme:** *Fine* also rhymes with *astronaut*—as long as it's delivered with conviction! ("I want to be a poet fine, because I am an astronaut!")

2. All of the learners will collaborate in extemporaneously composing a meaningful, spiritual, *rhyming* poem. The poem will be created out loud to the beat of a rigid, metric schedule imposed by everyone clapping together in time: 1-2-3-4. (Our advice: Some groups seem to have trouble keeping a beat. We recommend that you clap the beat yourself or use a metronome to help everyone keep time!) If at any point during the poem a poet's brain "fries," he or she is to produce a "So-sue-me" rhyme. The object is to deliver this "uh-oh" line with commitment—total commitment. Learners will find that this tends to win them as much applause as extemporizing the most brilliant, "perfect" rhyme. This realization should encourage them to start offering their spontaneous rhymes more and more freel. After all, they can't lose!

3. Ask all the learners to stand in a circle. Choose as the first volunteer whoever is wearing the most colorful clothes.

4. Ask the other learners to begin the rhyming beat by clapping.

5. You can start the first person off with a suggested line (Example: "I'm a poet with something to say"), or encourage the learner to come up with his or her own first line.

6. Go around the circle, with each person offering another line of the poem to the beat. Encourage the learners to talk without thinking. The objective is to practice the "So-sue-me" lines—not to rival Shakespeare. Continue until the poem is done, and then start a new poem.

7. If you have a small enough group, go around the circle for several rounds.

DEBRIEFING QUESTIONS

- How did it feel when you were "up"? What kind of pressure did you feel?

- What was it like to deliver your "So-sue-me" lines with pride and commitment? Were these lines funnier than the perfectly rhymed lines? If so, why? (Probably because they provided an *unexpected twist*, a key element of humor.)

- Why is it important for humorous people to be comfortable with the probability of screwing up? If you came up blank during a real presentation, what could you say or do? (Possible answer: Say, "I was going somewhere wonderful with that thought"—with conviction!)

- This game forced you to listen to the previously spoken line before responding. As trainers, how often do you truly wait to hear what a learner is saying before you respond? Why do we so often jump the gun? What's the impact of this on our learners?

- In what ways was this activity similar to real-life experiences you have had in delivering presentations? What are some insights about yourself that you had in this game? How could you apply these to your next training?

TIPS ON MAKING THIS GAME WORK WELL

Have your learners design their poems in pairs, simultaneously, without the added pressure of being observed by the rest of the group. If you choose this option, you should be the one who claps to establish the rhyming beat.

OTHER TOPICS THIS GAME TEACHES

- Creative Problem Solving
- Speaking Skills
- Team Building
- Reducing Workplace Negativity
- Icebreakers (Have a whole group stand in a circle and do one rhyming couplet after the other. For example, "It's nice to be with all of you," "I hope that you will like me, too," "Cuz if you don't, I'll run away," "And you'll be sorry—at least I hope so!")

GAME 3—PSYCHIC BUDDIES

THE POINT OF THIS GAME

Naturally funny people are **out-ward-focused**. This means they must listen carefully and be willing to adjust their preconceived ideas to support their partner's words and ideas. Contrast this perspective to inward-focused people, who essentially conduct a one-person monologue. The show may be polished and brilliant—but it's one in which in which *no one else gets to perform*. (Sadly, this describes the style of most stand-up comedians.)

Humorous people *involve* their audiences. Notice how some of the best comics in the business—Jonathan Winters, Robin Williams, and Paula Poundstone—frequently make their audiences a *big* part of the show. They stop and comment on what audience members are drinking or wearing; they ask them questions; they chat; sometimes they even bring them up onto the stage!

Trainers, too, can inspire their learners to "get on board" by generously sharing the spotlight with them. This game teaches a technique we call Letting Yourself Be Changed—loosening your hold on your own plans in order to better respond to your learners' ideas and comments.

TIME NEEDED

10–15 minutes

MATERIALS NEEDED

- An 8½ x 11-inch sheet of paper for each learner
- 3 x 5-inch index cards for each learner
- A pen or pencil for each learner

A SUGGESTED FUNNY INTRODUCTION

"Anyone here ever start a sentence, and your listener was so sure they knew what you were about to say that they cut in and finished it for you? [Show of hands] Raise your hand again if what *they* said was not what *you* were about to say! [Show of hands, laughter.]

"Okay, granted, this can be a bit annoying. But sometimes, if you're not married to your own ideas and are willing to *listen* to someone else's, it can be a gift. The willingness to incorporate other people's contributions makes the difference between a *monologue* and a *dialogue*. I call this Letting Yourself Be Changed. It's a great way for a trainer to get learners on board with you. Yet many trainers don't do it, often because their first reaction is the *annoyance* I mentioned earlier. Let's exercise this under-used muscle right now; what do you say?"

HOW TO PLAY THIS GAME

1. Ask your learners to think of three things they love to do as special treats for themselves, and to list them on three separate index cards. Ask them to be specific. For example, instead of writing down "Eating," learners should write "Japanese food"; instead of "Sports," they should write "baseball" or "hockey."

2. Underneath each activity, ask learners to list the main reasons *why* they enjoy this thing. For "Japanese food," reasons might be "Because it's so light and flavorful," or "Because it's always so beautifully presented," or "Because it's such a change from American food and I like variety," and so on. Have learners list all the reasons they can think of for liking what they like, *without showing what they've written to anyone else.*

3. Now ask learners to form pairs. Decide who of each pair has the smallest feet. That will be Person A.

4. Person A will play a famous psychic, using his or her amazing powers of intuition to guess the reason Partner B loves this activity. The problem is that as a psychic, Person A, well

... stinks. Often Person's A predictions have only a bizarre connection to the matter at hand.

5. Person B must on no account disagree with the psychic. Whatever the psychic states, Person B must accept whole-heartedly.

6. Person B starts off by looking at one of the cards and saying, perhaps, "I like ballroom dancing."

7. Immediately, Person A says, "Of *course* you do," and then goes on to provide a "weird" psychic intuition, "That's because ballroom dancers get to have such great snacks. And you love snacks. Especially Pop Tarts."

8. Person B must now agree with and confirm whatever the psychic buddy has just said, however bizarre. "Yes!" Person B might say: "It *is* a good way to work up an appetite and to meet people. In fact, I met my best friend Alice when we both went for the same Pop Tart during break."

9. Person A, the befuddled psychic, then makes another pro-nouncement, such as: "Your friend Alice prefers to snack on doggy biscuits."

10. Person B then confirms this response and continues the conversation. At any point, Person B can choose another activity card and ask the psychic to guess the reason why Person B loves *this* activity.

11. Give the pairs approximately 3 minutes for their dialogues, then switch roles. Person A chooses a card and says something like, "I like flying kites." Person B, the new befuddled psychic buddy, says, "Of *course* you do! That's because seagulls love to chase kites!" Person A replies, "Absolutely— I see many seagulls when I'm out with my kite. They seem to like blue colors the best."

12. Call time after 2 minutes.

DEBRIEFING QUESTIONS

- How difficult was it to abandon your own rationale and quick-ly think up something to say that would support your psychic partner's words? How do you generally respond when someone in real life doesn't "get" what you mean? What feelings come up?

- How did this activity allow you to practice your listening skills?

- What happens in your learning environment when a learner throws you a curve? How might you respond? What could you do to get other learners to help you? (Suggestion: "Anyone able to translate that for me?")

- What would it be like if everyone was always open to your ideas? How do you think people would perceive *you* if you were always open to theirs?

- **KEY POINT:** One of the best ways to be perceived as "fun" is to *make other people's ideas look good.* You don't have to abandon your own ideas, just put them on the back burner for the moment.

TIPS ON MAKING THIS GAME WORK WELL

This game can easily be adapted to teach communication and listening skills. You may want to have each pair go through a second round in which the psychic buddy strives to be on target

OTHER TOPICS THIS GAME TEACHES

- Creative Problem Solving
- Speaking Skills
- Team Building
- Emotional Intelligence
- Dealing with Change
- Reducing Workplace Negativity
- Dealing with Difficult People
- Management Skills
- Conflict and Negotiation
- Icebreaker

(Are you getting the idea that focusing outward is a universally useful skill? We certainly hope so.)

GAME 4—THE FORGETFUL STORYTELLER

THE POINT OF THIS GAME

Naturally funny people tend to **make positive choices**—they say "Yes!" to the world. Maybe this is why they come up with more humorous ideas, since neuroscientific studies have shown that both cognitive and creative thinking improve dramatically when mental imagery, and subsequent emotions, are positive. Anyway, their habitual positivity makes other people feel good, and this alone is an excellent reason to cultivate it.

TIME NEEDED

15–20 minutes

MATERIALS NEEDED

None

A SUGGESTED FUNNY INTRODUCTION

"I have a small sign on my kitchen wall that expresses my mental state perfectly. It says:

"'I can't remember why I came in here.' Darned if that sign doesn't become more and more appropriate as years go by! How many here could use such a sign? [Show of hands.] So I'm not the only one who goes through that—thank heaven! Well, now that we've established that we're all a bit forgetful, I'm confident you'll be very good at this next game."

HOW TO PLAY THIS GAME

1. Have your learners form pairs and, in each pair, decide who is wearing the brightest colors or the boldest patterns. That will be Person A.

2. Person A asks Person B for a title of a story that's never been written. Person B must offer something negative (For example, "Alone and Unloved" or "My Night in Jail"). Person A now begins to tell an extemporaneous story based on the title. At various points throughout the story, Person A stops, looks at Person B, and says, "I forget the next part." Person B then fills in whatever comes to mind, as long as it's unpleasant. For example:

   Person A: "Alone and Unloved," by I. M. Paranoid.* Once upon a time there was a miserable, bitter old woman named … hmm, I forget her name—

   Person B: Mrs. Scab.

   Person A Yes, Mrs. Scab. Old Mrs. Scab hated people. She hated them because … I forget why—

   Person B: Because they had always been horrible to her.

   Person A: That's right. Nobody had ever been kind to her. One day, she decided to get back at the world. She decided to … hmm—

   Person B: Go out and dig up people's flower beds.

   Person A: Yes! Out she went in the dead of night, armed with a spade …

   You get the idea. Carry on until the story reaches some logical conclusion.

3. Now Person A asks Person B for another title, this time an agreeable one. Person B says something like, "The Happy Little Campers." Person A begins anew, with Person B this time adding positive details. Continue until the story is finished.

*Note: Author' name is optional.

14

DEBRIEFING QUESTIONS

- Both stories probably made the two of you laugh. Was there any difference in the *quality* of the laughter from one story to the next?

- Did you notice any difference in the pacing of the two stories? (For example, did Person B have more ideas, or come up with them faster, the first time or the second?)

- Were there any differences in your body language from one story to the next? If so, why?

- Which story went on longer?

- The observations you make in this game will probably be fairly subtle. First, in both stories you were playing around with creativity, and creativity is always exhilarating, so both stories probably generated energy. Second, you might possibly have laughed harder while telling your negative story! This can easily happen, because humor is largely about things going wrong. Still, it is likely that the happy story gave you both more overall *animation*—you went on longer, moved faster, perhaps got more uproariously silly, and felt more as if you were both on the same wavelength.

- In real life, does your outlook reflect a positive or negative perspective? How would your solutions differ if you focused on opportunity-naming instead of problem-solving?

- Think about how you debrief or conduct process questioning after leading learners through an activity. What would be positive questions to ask? How would you characterize a positive question?

TIPS ON MAKING THIS GAME WORK WELL

Your learners should not try to be funny, and definitely not try to be original! If their story is about a witch, they should make her fly on a broomstick, have a gingerbread house, a cauldron for boiling up little boys and girls, and all the standard accouterments. If it's about a cowboy, they should have him ride a horse, sit around campfires, rope cows. You get the idea.

OTHER TOPICS THIS GAME TEACHES

- Creative Problem Solving
- Speaking Skills
- Management Skills
- Reducing Workplace Negativity
- Dealing with Difficult People
- Conflict and Negotiation

GAME 5—BOMB WITH APLOMB

THE POINT OF THIS GAME

Naturally humorous trainers accept that, sooner or later, a workshop won't go as well as expected. They respond to these "unfunny" moments with comments and insights that **acknowledge the bomb**, allowing their learners to remain relaxed and positive.

TIME NEEDED

15 minutes

MATERIALS

- One or more oddly shaped items, such as a plunger, colander, dart, or electric toothbrush
- Flip chart paper

A SUGGESTED FUNNY INTRODUCTION

"In the world of comedy, there is one word that makes everybody sit up and take notice: bombing. Bombing means telling a joke no one laughs at. This is an experience every professional comic seeks rigorously to avoid.

"Trainers also understand bombing. In our world, it happens whenever our delivery doesn't have the desired effect. Maybe we mispronounce a word with rather embarrassing consequences. Maybe our PowerPoint presentation crashes. Maybe that exercise we planned so carefully wasn't effective, or pushed emotional buttons we didn't anticipate. Maybe one or more learners came into the learning environment with hostility, and began to challenge or even sabotage us.

"It makes good sense to try to avoid bombing, but it is foolish to fear it. Comedians, trainers, and anyone else who fears bombing have simply forgotten the intrinsic nature of humor. They think it offers no room for error. Naturally humorous people, on the other hand, instinctively know and accept one thing: *Sooner or later, everyone bombs.* They also know how to come out of a bomb smelling like a rose. Which you will also know in just a moment. But first, let's make the distinction between a *bomb* and an *error.*

"An error is something that causes pain or embarrassment to *someone else.* A bomb is something that causes *only* embarrassment, and only to *you.* Naturally humorous people offer sincere apologies for their *errors,* and cheerfully acknowledge their *bombs*—usually with a funny comment. "I really do have a sense of humor," one may say, "just not a good one." Or: "I do have standards, you know—they're just not high." Or: "I don't trust anyone who can't spell a word more than one way."

"If you didn't know this before, it is time you found out: *Many so-called ad libs, in comedy clubs or presidential speeches, are planned in advance.* This is because professional communicators know that 1) bombing happens, and 2) acknowledging the bomb is just too important a strategy to leave to chance. Comedians write their own ad libs. Politicians, of course, have their speechwriters do it. But one way or another, they all prepare them. It's time you wrote one for yourself.

HOW TO PLAY THIS GAME

1. Brainstorm with your learners responses you could make if you bombed in front of a group. Start your learners off with a few suggestions, such as: "Please, hold your applause—there's lots more where that came from" or "I know—amazing wasn't it?" or "I'll take that corner office now." Record all possible responses on flip chart paper.

2. Now teach your learners the "Clown Bow" response. When all else fails, the Clown Bow means facing your group, smiling

modestly and saying, "Thank you, Thank you very much."
(*Note:* You do not actually have to bow to do the clown bow.
You simply have to cheerfully pretend that instead of just
bombing, you are acknowledging wild, enthusiastic applause.)

3. Encourage your learners to try a few variations of the Clown
    Bow. They can say it soulfully, like a diva. They can say it en-
    thusiastically, like a radio personality. They can say it like Elvis
    if they want to. They can say it till they've found their own
    personal style, the one that makes their own eyes twinkle.

4. Now show the oddly shaped object to the group. The pur-
    pose of this game is to come up with alternate uses for the
    object.

5. Line your group up in either one long line or two lines fac-
    ing toward the front of the room. Learners will run to the
    front of the room, pick up the object, "name" the object and
    describe it's use, and then run to the back of the line.

6. At any point, a learner who brain-fries or blanks out can use
    one of the phrases just brainstormed by the group or do the
    Clown Bow. In fact, since the skill they are practicing here is
    bombing with aplomb, they do not need to be very creative
    for this game.

DEBRIEFING QUESTIONS

-   Ask yourself: Is there any likelihood that you might make a
    mistake at any time in the next three days? If you answered
    "yes," give yourself the assignment of using your ad lib and
    seeing how people respond. I think you will be impressed—
    and will start to lose all fear of this inevitable, and very human,
    experience.

-   [Comedy line: "If you answered 'no' to the first question,
    please stay behind after this workshop. I'd be fascinated to talk
    to you."]

-   **KEY POINT:** Like everything else in life, it's not whether
    you fall, but how you land, that counts.

OTHER TOPICS THIS GAME TEACHES

- Assertiveness
- Creative Problem Solving
- Facilitation Skills
- Management Skills
- Reducing Workplace Negativity
- Customer Service

2

Five Games to Enhance Creative Thinking and Problem-Solving Skills

The games in this chapter have been designed to build sequentially by topic and risk level. We recommend that you play the games in the order in which they are presented here.

GAME 1—NUMBERS DON'T LIE

THE POINT OF THIS GAME

People who are considered creative **don't take creativity too seriously!** This is because they understand a fundamental truth about the creative process: You've got to go through a lot of lousy ideas before you get to a good one.

People who accept this truth explore new mental frontiers with avid curiosity. They take chances. They boldly go where no one has gone before, just for the heck of it. They make mistakes—and have a lot of fun doing so.

And what's the usual result? They get to the gold, more often and more quickly than the rest of us, who hesitate and dally, constantly evaluating and editing our ideas before we dare even speak them aloud.

In this game, your learners will practice the fine art of Making Mistakes with Glee. This is far more than just a technique; it is a *state of mind*. It is vital that your learners get firmly into this state of mind now, as it will help them to unleash their creativity in the exercises to follow—to really *play* with ideas.

TIME NEEDED

15–20 minutes

MATERIALS NEEDED

• None

A SUGGESTED FUNNY INTRODUCTION

"I'd like to see a show of hands: Has anyone here ever … *made a mistake*? [Raise your own hand.] Anyone? Or is it just me? [Your learners will raise their hands and laugh. Some wag might say something like, "Once I thought I made a mistake, but I was wrong." Be sure to give some sort of "Yes, *and*" response: "Wow, *that* must have been embarrassing. Don't let *that* happen too often …!"]

"Well. So we've all made mistakes. Hey—has anyone here made *more than one*? [Show of hands, laughter.] Well, fancy that …

"Hey! Anyone think you might just make *one more mistake* sometime before you die? [Show of hands.] Gee. Who would have thought …?

"Did you know that every 'creative genius' on this planet—Thomas Edison, Martha Graham, Walt Disney, Albert Einstein—has had far more unworkable ideas than workable ones? The only difference between these people and the rest of us is that *they kept on taking risks*. They knew they wouldn't find any brilliant new ideas by going down the same old mental paths. Too many others have gone down those paths; those paths are picked clean.

"If we want to be creative, we have to catch up with these geniuses. I'm not saying that we should *try* to make mistakes. I'm saying we must be *willing to*—agreed? Okay. That means we have to start cutting ourselves—and others—a little more slack than we usually do. Here's a game to help us do just that. Please, stand up!"

HOW TO PLAY THIS GAME

1. The group stands in a horseshoe formation. Count off down the line so that each player has a number.

2. The first person (Number 1 in the lineup) calls out someone else's number: "Twelve!" That person immediately calls out someone else's number: "Five!" That person quickly calls out

another number: "Eight!" and so on. The first person to hesitate at all, or call a wrong number (either their own or one that doesn't exist), relinquishes his or her place and goes to the end of the line. That person and all who were previously behind him or her in the lineup *now have different numbers*. The game resumes.

3. As it continues, people will constantly "blow it" and have to move to the end of the line. But here's the hitch: Rather than grimacing or groaning, they must raise one fist into the air and say "Yes!" with triumph, and trot proudly to last place. Everyone else must applaud admiringly.

4. Call time after about 5 minutes.

DEBRIEFING QUESTIONS

- How did it feel to make light of minor failure? How did it feel to watch someone else do it?

- Why are we usually inclined to gnash our teeth and groan when we fail—even in (let's face it) a silly little game that has no bearing on real life?

- **KEY POINT:** Are there any other minor failures you have made too much of in your life?

- The "Yes!" is a device that essentially puts a mistake into perspective. When you say, in effect, "Didn't I do that *well?*" everyone understands you really mean, "Whoops, won't do that again! And now let's move on." What are some other ways to convey this humorously besides throwing your arms up and saying, "Yes!"? [Possible answers include: "Thank you, that took years of training," "Please, hold your applause," "May I pause just to savor this moment?" **KEY POINT:** The best "Yes's" use gentle, positive, turn-about humor.]

- What concerns do you have about using "Yes" in real life? (Possible answer: The "Yes" is inappropriate for really serious mistakes. Your response: Agree, and then clarify the difference between *minor* and *major* mistakes. Major mistakes cause pain or loss, or embarrassment for *others*. Minor mistakes cause *only* embarrassment, and only for *you.* Remind them how it felt to watch each other deal lightheartedly with minor mistakes in this game. Saying "Yes!" relieved everyone present of the burden of feeling unnecessarily uncomfortable on their team member's behalf. After all, that person had only done what all people do from time to time—made a minor mistake. Big deal!)

TIPS ON MAKING THIS GAME WORK WELL

Keep the pace so fast that everybody (including you) "fails" a lot! Besides giving them lots of practice in saying "Yes" (providing, by the way, a great bonding experience), this will also help get them into a bold, pleasurable, "no fear" state of mind for the more advanced creativity games later in this chapter.

OTHER TOPICS THIS GAME TEACHES

- Assertiveness
- How to Be a Naturally Funny Trainer
- Speaking Skills

GAME 2—BRAIN FRY

THE POINT OF THIS GAME

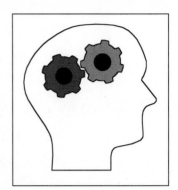

Creative people deliver breakthrough ideas because they know how to **break out of their habitual paths of thought**. The Brain Fry game is designed to get your learners' brains to short-circuit old neural channels—literally forging new electrical pathways in their brains. We suggest that you use the Brain Fry game as warm-up to help your learners limber up neurologically for any problem-solving, planning, or brainstorming activity you lead. A rousing round of Brain Fry is ideal for the beginning of any meeting, workshop, or retreat to encourage new perspectives and insights.

TIME NEEDED

10 minutes

MATERIALS NEEDED

None

A SUGGESTED FUNNY INTRODUCTION

"How many have ever known someone who was *highly creative*? [Show of hands.] How many noticed that sometimes this person had ideas or said things that seemed a *little bit crazy*? [Show of hands.]

"It's true: Creativity sometimes looks a little crazy. But that's because the only way to get really unique ideas is to break away from so-called normal thinking. So if we want to be more creative today ... we're all going to have to get a little more crazy!

"What do you say—who wants to get crazy?

"Only a couple people? Too bad! *Everybody* up!"

HOW TO PLAY THIS GAME

1. Tell your learners to pick a number between one and three. Have them hold up that many fingers. Now tell them to quickly find three other people who are holding up the same number of fingers.

2. Once everyone is in a team of four people, tell them to pick the team member with the smallest eyebrows. That person will be the first Target Person. Next have teams quickly pick the people who go second, third, and fourth.

3. Have the first Target Person stand facing the team, who now act as the Firing Line. When you say, "Go!" the Firing Line, *in rapid succession,* will shout out single words to their cohort: "Sky!" "Chair!" "Freckle!" The words can be anything at all, but to each one, the cohort must *immediately* respond with another word: "Blue!" "Grandma!" "Sun!" (*Note:* The response words do not need to relate in any way to the words shouted; they need only to be *immediate.*) The Target Person must go on till his or her brain fries, meaning the person suddenly can't think of any response words quickly. As soon as you find yourself saying, "Oh, um, ah …" you must announce, "I'm fried," and do a "Yes!" You then take the last person's place in the Firing Line, and the game resumes.

4. Go on until everyone in the team has had at least one turn as the Target Person. Then have the learners return to their seats.

DEBRIEFING QUESTIONS

Since this is a warm-up technique, no discussion is needed. Just ask your learners if they feel a little *crazier* than they did five minutes ago. They will probably laugh and nod emphatically. Lead them in a final: "Yes! Thank you. Now we can do some really outstanding work." Move directly on to the next game while their brains are still "warmed up."

TIPS ON MAKING THIS GAME WORK WELL

The main thing is to keep the game moving *fast*. Keep monitoring the teams throughout. If any Target Person slows down at all (typically this will come in the form of, "Ummmmm, *horse!*"), congratulate the person on having fried and invite him or her to step down at once. Be sure to reinforce the "Yes" technique.

Depending on time, team members can each take more than one turn at being the Target Person.

GAME 3—FREE ASSOCIATION

THE POINT OF THIS GAME

Believe it or not, people who are considered creative usually **don't try to be original** in coming up with ideas! How can this be?

First, because they discovered long ago that *many of the best ideas spring from very unoriginal sources.* Second and more important, they know that in taxing their brains to come up with one original idea after another, they quickly become stressed and tired, ultimately causing their creativity to grind to a disheartening halt.

Many great ideas have come from mundane sources. (For example, needing a book mark for a choir book led to the development of Post-It notes.) How often have problem-solvers said, "The solution was right in front of us all the time"?

The rule of creative thinking is: *Generate* the ideas first; *evaluate* them later.

A SUGGESTED FUNNY INTRODUCTION

"We've already seen how many of us have made mistakes. How many have ever had an *unoriginal idea*? [Show of hands.] Wow—that many? Great! Looks like we'll *excel* at this next game. ..."

TIME NEEDED

15 minutes

MATERIALS NEEDED

A flip chart, whiteboard, or overhead projector

HOW TO PLAY THIS GAME

1. Have your learners come up with a goal or objective they need to fulfill. It could be "better customer relations," "more accurately filled out forms," "more employee involvement in the company newsletter," or whatever.

2. Write the objective in the center of the flip chart, whiteboard, or overhead, preferably on a diagonal slant.*

3. Have the learners start calling out any and all words or phrases that occur to them regarding this objective. Firmly instruct them not to be original, but just to share whatever words come to them. For example, if the objective is "more employee involvement in the company newsletter," typical words and phrases might include: Interest, excitement, communicating ideas, sharing ownership, gossip articles, announcements, etc. But someone may call out, "Breathe easier!" *Write it down.* This person may be the editor of the newsletter, and might indeed breathe easier if there was more active participation from employees. The main thing is for people to keep coming up with words—*and fast*—until they run out. Write down everything they say.

4. When the group has exhausted its storehouse of words, stop. Look over what you've got, and select whatever word or phrase most interests you and the group, for whatever reason. Write this down in the middle of a new flip chart page.

5. Repeat Steps 3 and 4 two to five times. The idea is to take the group further and further off on a tangent. Continually remind them of the original objective. Keep going until you hit gold, or stumble upon a concept that relates to your objective, and is—yes—original! Have the group give themselves a hand when they accomplish this.

*People seem to more quickly break out of old patterns of thought when familiar activities are done in unfamiliar ways—like not writing a title horizontally at the top of a page! In teaching creativity, do what you can to subtly throw a curve at your learners. Play music during exercises or to signal breaks, display posters of poems and quotes, lead half-hourly stretch breaks, have them change seats or partners regularly, etc.

DEBRIEFING QUESTIONS

- Why did this process work? That is, how did we come up with original ideas when we weren't trying to be original? [Answer: We tried to have *lots* of ideas, not original ones.]
- What keeps most people from having more original ideas? [Answer: They don't stay with it—they quit when their ideas seem to be going nowhere.]
- What have you learned about originality?
- **KEY POINT:** Are *you* an original, innovative person? [Answer: *Yes!*]

TIPS ON MAKING THIS GAME WORK WELL

Note: People often feel a bit intimidated the first time they play idea-generation games. This is because most of us *do* believe we're "just not creative" (read: *original*). Using a funny introduction is particularly recommended for this game, since laughter seems to dispel feelings of intimidation like magic.

You yourself will lead this game with more confidence if you have first played it once or twice, with fellow trainers, with family members, or even with friends at a party! (Yes, it's a *great* party game, easily as much fun as Charades or Trivial Pursuit. Just pick a generally-experienced problem, like "Get the kids to go to bed on time," or "Make government employees more helpful," and go to town!) Having played What's Inside? (Chapter 1), Group Mind Story (Chapter 4), or Phrase Ball (Chapter 6) will also give you more facility—and faith—in the capricious, startling, *wondrous* nature of the creative process—a process we were all born to use!

In Step 1, it's best to set an objective that isn't too emotionally charged. For example, at this stage in their creativity training, an objective like "Stop office gossip and backbiting" might overwhelm learners with the perceived magnitude of the task, inhibiting them from approaching it with optimism. (After all, gossip and backbiting are behaviors that seem well entrenched in many organizations! As such, they tend to inspire a level of hopelessness that can scuttle creativity in the early stages.) Save these kinds of challenging objectives until after your learners get a few wins under their belts.

In Step 3, definitely do *not* pause to give quizzical or pained looks to any learner who makes a *non sequitur* offering (like "Breathe easier!" in the example). This will only retard the idea-generation process at this point. Remember that many times it's exactly these kinds of weird contributions that can jog a group outside its "box," spurring it on to unexpected and new mental associations.

GAME 4—RANDOM ACCESS

THE POINT OF THIS GAME

People who are considered creative seldom pull imaginative new
ideas out of thin air. More often
they stumble upon them, so to
speak, by **making unexpected
connections** between *old* ideas.

How do they accomplish this,
especially if, as we said in Game 3,
they don't try to be original?

The secret lies in the word *try*. People who are considered
creative don't pressure themselves to make innovative new connections. They just open their eyes (and minds) to the world
around them, then wait expectantly for it to fork over the
goods. And, surprise of surprises, the world is usually remarkably
cooperative!

This game will give your learners a powerful (and extremely fun) technique for getting the world to fork over the
goods.

TIME NEEDED

You can take anything from 15 minutes for a simple practice of
this idea-generation technique, to over 45 minutes if you use it
to actually problem-solve with your group.

MATERIALS NEEDED

- An overhead or flip chart
- A dictionary or other book, magazine, or newspaper

A SUGGESTED FUNNY INTRODUCTION

"First question: How many have ever thought, 'I'm just not a creative person. I have other talents—I grow healthy houseplants, I

can sing, I'm a good parent, I make great zucchini bread. ... But creative? Nope. Not me.' [Show of hands.]

"Second question: How many here are ... *former children?* Anyone? [Show of hands, laughter.]

"Well, if you're a former child, you're a naturally creative person. I'll prove it. How many have kids? [Show of hands.] Tell me: If you gave your kids, say, a garden hose, would they start watering the garden? [Laughter from parents and non-parents alike.] No, indeed! What would that garden hose become? A snake ... a whip ... [Let your learners join in. They will enjoy coming up with things like: a jump rope; a harness for chariot horses; cursive letters; a rope to tie up the bad guy with; a Safety Zone demarcation line for playing tag, etc., etc.]

"That's right. The *last* thing any self-respecting kid would do is use that hose the way it was intended. That's called *play.* And play is creativity. Play and creativity are the same thing because both involve *finding unexpected connections between things.*

"And of course if you're a former child, you were *born* knowing how to play. That means you're naturally good at making unexpected connections—you're naturally creative! So what do you say we get back in touch with that natural creativity right now? Great. Let's go."

HOW TO PLAY THIS GAME

1. Have the group decide on an objective. Examples: "Increase employee retention," "Bring in new customers," "Improve productivity." Write the objective out at the top of the flip chart or overhead.

2. Now open the book or magazine, cover your eyes, and point to a spot on the page. Whatever word you're touching is the word your group will use for this exercise. (*Note:* If you landed on an article or a connecting word—*the, is, and,* etc.— choose a word next to it.) Write the word at the bottom of the flip chart.

3. Instruct the group that you will all seek to find as many relationships as possible between the word you chose and the group's objective.

4. Start off by modeling the process yourself. Let's say the objective is to increase retention of good employees, and the word you landed on was *bunny*. Begin free-associating out loud: "Hm, bunnies, rabbits, rabbit hutches, carrots—use a carrot instead of a stick, more rewards and fewer threats? [Write this down.] What else? Nibbling, wiggling noses—hm, Samantha on *Bewitched*? Witchcraft, magic, keeping your mortal husband from losing his temper? Hm, a temper-tantrum room right next to the coffee room? [Write it down.] Or—we're *all* mortal, all human, we all have a lot in common ... finding more commonality—team building? [Write it down.] Back to the bunnies. Playboy—whoops! Well, it's worth looking at for a moment: Bunny of the Year, Employee of the Year, more celebration and appreciation for work well done? [Write it down.] The Easter Bunny! Painted eggs, Easter egg hunts ...."

   You get the idea. Constantly pause to look around, inviting input from the group. They will quickly get the idea and begin to respond. (To further ensure this, see Tips.)

5. If, after at least *one minute of sincere effort*—and no less—you and your learners don't come up with much, you may now discard the word and pick another one. Go until the group has come up with at least several promising ideas (ideas that need more development), or one "keeper."

DEBRIEFING QUESTIONS

- What did we just do differently from the way we *usually* try to come up with new ideas?
- How did it feel to go off the beaten path—to consider and play with ideas that didn't always make sense at the outset? Was it uncomfortable?
- Did you become more comfortable with this uncertainty as the game went on?

- **KEY POINT:** How likely are you to find really innovative ideas if you play it safe—that is, approach the problem logically or make sensible (read: *traditional*) connections?

TIPS ON MAKING THIS GAME WORK WELL

An outstanding way to ease your learners' inhibitions is to start off leading the group in a playfully solemn vow: "For the benefit of the group, and in the spirit of large-hearted generosity, I pledge to proudly contribute even my *stupid* ideas to this process." Why is it important for them to feel comfortable about sharing not-so-good ideas? Because 1) in creativity, stupid ideas *often* lead to good ones; 2) sometimes they only *seem* stupid at first, but are actually winners; and 3) because by allowing themselves to make *minor failures* in public (see Game 1), each learner gives permission to peers to take the same risk.

To further facilitate this, *be sure to share lots of bad ideas as you model this game at the start!* We can't overemphasize this tip: You will embolden your learners to join in more quickly and freely if they see that even the teacher is allowed to be less than brilliant. Do it lightheartedly. Say: "Hey, I've got a *really stupid* one!" Share your idea, then look around expectantly, and make some motion inviting applause. When your learners give it to you, duck your head modestly and say, "Thank you. You're too kind. No, please—stop," or some such. After you've done this once or twice, your learners will get the idea. Don't be surprised when they start to raise *their* hands excitedly and say, "*I've got a really stupid one!*" Lead the admiring applause, then enthusiastically write the idea down. Then watch as the ideas start pouring forth, getting you all to your goal faster than you would have dreamed!

OTHER TOPICS THIS GAME TEACHES

- Team Building
- Dealing with Change

GAME 5—PLAYBOOK

THE POINT OF THIS GAME

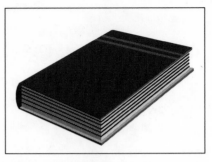

People who are considered creative show extraordinary **mental flexibility**. Yes, they are willing to examine and play with even crazy-sounding ideas (if only for a moment). But if an idea doesn't seem to be working, they promptly let it go, confident that there will be plenty more where that one came from. Their secret is that they remain open to possibilities and are able to adapt to the changing environment around them.

TIME NEEDED

20 minutes

MATERIALS NEEDED

- A playbook (i.e., the script of a play). These are available at drama bookstores or at your local library. *Our Town* or musicals like *Oklahoma* or *The Music Man* are usually readily available, and are excellent for this game. Many other plays work equally well. Just be sure to pick one that 1) is generally positive in nature, and 2) uses colloquial language. (In other words, Greek plays and Shakespeare are out!)
- An Observation Checklist (see handout) for each of the learners who will watch this game

A SUGGESTED FUNNY INTRODUCTION

"How many have ever been to Las Vegas? [Show of hands.] Anyone play blackjack or poker? [Show of hands.] How many were allowed to request which cards you wanted from the dealer? [Show of hands.] No one? Hm.

"Think about it: Life is a lot like a Las Vegas blackjack dealer—it doesn't take requests. And just as in poker, success often isn't in the cards you're dealt, but... [Let them fill in:] that's right, *how you play your hand.*

"Let's practice turning an unexpected hand into a winning hand."

HOW TO PLAY THIS GAME

1. Select two volunteers by announcing, "I need two people who took acting classes back in college or high school." Wait for hands to go up. If none do, then say, "Okay, I need two people who *considered* taking acting in college or high school." If still no hands go up, say, "All right, I need two people who ever lied to get off the phone." When the hands shoot up, pick two and say, "You're natural actors! Come on down!"

2. Have your learners come up with a typical business scenario involving two people. (Examples: a customer service rep assisting a customer; two colleagues working together on a project; a salesperson pitching a product.)

3. Find out which of your two players brought the most writing instruments (pens, pencils, highlighters, whatever) to the workshop. This will be Person A, and the other Person B. Give Person B the playbook, turned to a page where there are lots of short lines of dialogue. (Note: It's best to have this page flagged before the outset of the game.)

4. Briefly demonstrate the game with Person B, using three or four lines of dialogue from, say, *Ah, Wilderness!* by Eugene O'Neill. For example, you may begin:

   "Thank you for calling XYZ Company. How may I help you?"

   Your partner now turns to a page and reads: "Oh, hello, is it nine already? Gosh, time passes—when you're thinking."

   Respond as if this line makes perfect sense in the context of a customer service rep talking with a customer: "Well, whatever you're thinking about, I'm sure I can help you. To whom am I speaking?" (Remember what you learned in Game 1: Don't take this too seriously! You don't have to be brilliantly witty—you have only to *connect with* what your partner just read, in any way at all. It's the connection that will get the laughs.)

Your partner now reads the next line of dialogue from the book: "I thought you'd be waiting right here at the end of the path. I'll bet you'd forgotten I was even coming." You answer, perhaps: "Oh, are you outside? You must be calling from one of our cell phones. How's it working for you?"

Person B now reads: "No, I hadn't forgotten, honest. But I got to thinking about life." You respond with something like: "Well, cell phones are certainly making life more convenient," or whatever.

5. Now set your two actors loose to improvise their scenario, with Person A constantly adapting to Person B's prewritten *non sequiturs*. Stress to Person A that his or her job is *only* to connect to what Person B says. Remind the actors that if they are stumped at any point in the scenario, they can get help from the audience.

6. After 3 to 5 minutes, call time and lead a walloping round of applause for the actors (see Tips). Invite them to go back to their seats.

DEBRIEFING QUESTIONS

- Lead the observers through the questions on the Observation Checklist.

- To Person A: How did it feel to have to keep changing gears— adapting the conversation to these unexpected comments? [Answer: Some people will say they enjoyed this, while others will have found it irksome. **KEY POINT:** The difference seems to lie in a natural human desire, stronger in some of us than in others, to know what's coming next—to cling to the security of the *predictable*.]

- Will we get many new ideas if we cling to predictability?

- How can we get better at letting go of predictability?
- To Person A: What tricks seemed to help *you* let go of your expectations and go with the flow? When did you find it hardest to be flexible? Why do you think that was so?
- To Person B: How did it feel when Person A made your comments work in the context of the scenario?
- **KEY POINT:** What if all our coworkers tried to think of ways to make our ideas work before discarding them?

TIPS ON MAKING THIS GAME WORK WELL

When leading applause after this game, point first to Person A, who will undoubtedly get a rousing hand for sportsmanship. Next, point to Person B, and say, "And *what* a performance! So fast on the feet; never once needed coaching from the audience! Come on, let's hear it!" This will get a huge laugh and, very likely, good-natured whoops and cheers. Don't be surprised if Person B bows and waves like a homecoming hero.*

OTHER TOPICS THIS GAME TEACHES

- Team Building
- How to Be a Naturally Funny Trainer
- Speaking Skills
- Customer Service

*Don't worry that this will make Person A feel undervalued. Everyone in the room will know which player had the *really* challenging role in this game. This is merely a bit of turnabout humor that will allow both people to enjoy their contributions equally. And both contributions *were*, of course, equally important!

OBSERVATION CHECKLIST

1. Which of Person B's comments seemed most *easily adapted* into the scenario?

2. Which seemed most difficult to adapt? Why do you think that was so?

3. Did Person A seem to get better at the task as the game progressed?

4. In your opinion, which was the most successful (interesting, innovative, funny, etc.) of Person A's adaptations? Why?

3

Five Games to Create Intrinsically Motivating Managers

GAME 1—ALPHA LEADERS

THE POINT OF THIS GAME

Effective managers **adapt their style to the needs of their employees and the situation.** This game identifies some defining qualities of various leadership styles, and helps managers define the qualities of their own styles.

TIME NEEDED

40–60 minutes

MATERIALS NEEDED

- 'Alpha Leaders' portraits* (or, if not possible, their names) posted around the room, approximately 2–5 feet apart on 8½ × 11-inch sheets of paper.

  You can use any or all of the following Alpha Leaders: Moses, Abraham Lincoln, Joan of Arc, Eleanor Roosevelt, Mahatma Ghandi, Christopher Columbus, Queen Elizabeth I, Winston Churchill, Oprah Winfrey, the Ayatollah Khomeini, Mr. Rogers, Attila the Hun. (Note: Feel free to include or substitute any others you like better. The point here is to have a range of style orientations: people vs. task, thinking vs. doing, passive vs.

*Using *portraits* instead of just names will aid learning in two ways. First, the brain naturally thinks in pictures, so information delivered visually is almost guaranteed to be more long-lasting. Second, this game will feel funnier to your learners if you *hand-draw* portraits of these famous people. Note that your depictions do *not* have to be realistic—in fact your learners will get a bigger kick out of truly badly-drawn portraits! Just make sure the name of the person is prominent on the portrait. (If you're a die-hard Type A, you can always get original pictures from magazines, textbooks, encyclopedias, the Web or almost anywhere. Enlarge them on the copy machine, tape them up on a window, and trace them. Your learners will be *so* impressed!)

aggressive, and so on. You may also want to pick leaders who are specific to your industry and familiar to your learners.)

- A blank piece of flip chart paper posted next to each portrait
- An Alpha Leaders worksheet for each learner
- Two small voting slips for each learner (1 x 3-inch hand-torn pieces of paper will do fine)
- A pen or pencil for each learner

A SUGGESTED FUNNY INTRODUCTION

"In dog packs, there's always one dog that is recognized by the other dogs as the Big Cheese. This is the dog that is the *sniffer* and not the *sniffee*, if you get my drift—the Alpha dog. We have the same concept in human packs, except without all the unsightly sniffing. Alpha Leader is a term describing a person who, through some combination of skills, personality, and timing, has become a cultural icon. Obviously, not all of us can be Alpha Leaders—too many chefs will ruin the soup. But anyone who leads groups of people must be curious: How did these leaders accomplish what they did? How did they get people motivated? Get everyone on the same page? Make sure information was clearly communicated down the ranks? Find out what people in the bottom ranks were thinking and doing? Stop people from whining when things got tough?

"And most of all ... how did they make sure staff members didn't sniff anyone? Studies show that's just not good business practice."

HOW TO PLAY THIS GAME

1. Distribute the Alpha Leaders worksheets to your learners. Ask them to match a leader on the wall to each question on the worksheet. They can name the same leader more than once. When they have completed the worksheet, ask your learners to hold their pens in the air.

2. Tell the group that they will now get to see which Alpha Leaders their colleagues chose. Read each question aloud, and ask your learners to stand underneath the portrait of their chosen Alpha Leader.

3. Ask your learners to describe why they chose this leader. Record the reasons on the flip chart paper posted next to the portrait.

4. Repeat this process for each question.

5. Ask your learners to be seated. Select the two or three portraits that were chosen most often by the learners during the activity.

6. Ask the group to review the comments written about those leaders on the flip chart paper and to come up with a characteristic quote each leader might make on the nature of management. The quote might start out with: "Always remember ..." or "Good managers ...". Write the group's favorite quote underneath the appropriate leader's portrait.

DEBRIEFING QUESTIONS

- Were there any surprises over which Alpha Leaders were chosen? [Possible answers: Your learners might have deemed Attila the Hun's style desirable in a crisis; conversely, everyone may have wanted Mr. Rogers as an *uncle*, but might not have wanted him in charge of an important operation! This can be illuminating to many learners, who might have believed that one style—usually theirs—was appropriate for all situations.]

- Was any Alpha Leader chosen most often? If so, why do you think that was? If not, did any of the Alpha Leaders have *qualities in common*, and did any of these qualities come up *often* in choosing a leader? [This will give your learners some insight into qualities that seem most universally attractive—qualities they themselves might wish to develop or improve upon.]

- What insights do you have about different leadership or management styles?

- Is there a difference between being a *leader* and being a *manager*? In other words, do any of the Alpha *Leaders* possess weaknesses that might get in the way of being effective *managers*?
- **KEY POINT:** Which of the leaders might be good at handling supervisory problems *you yourself face*?
- What insights did you have about your own style and preferences?
- You've just identified how different styles would suit *your* workplace. Would your answers have changed for *other* workplaces? How is your workplace different from some others?
- **KEY POINT:** If your employees were to stand under *your* portrait in an Alpha Leader activity, what would they see as your qualities? In what situations might they choose a different Alpha Leader?
- **A VERY INTERESTING KEY POINT:** What barriers (both internal and external) do you face that prevent you from being the type of leader you would like to be?
- Based on this insight, what can you do differently in how you work?

TIPS ON MAKING THIS GAME WORK WELL

With a large group of participants, you may want to reduce the number of questions the learners will respond to or allow the learners to stay seated when naming their Alpha Leaders.

OTHER TOPICS THIS GAME TEACHES

- Personality Inventory
- Dealing with Difficult People
- Values
- Conflict and Negotiation

ALPHA LEADERS WORKSHEET

HANDOUT

Directions: Alpha Leader is a term describing a person who, through some combination of skills, personality, and timing, has become a *cultural icon of his or her period.* Some Alpha Leaders are listed below. You will probably recognize most (or all) of them.

Obviously, not all of us can be Alpha Leaders. But anyone who leads groups of people must be curious: *How did these leaders accomplish what they did?* How did they get people motivated? Get everyone on the same page? Make sure information was clearly communicated down the ranks? Find out what people in the bottom ranks were thinking and doing? Stop people from whining when things got tough?

Choose one leader from the following list for each of the following categories. Your choice of leader should be based on your own personal sense of that leader's qualities, skills, and leadership style.

Some Alpha Leaders:

Abraham Lincoln, Joan of Arc, Eleanor Roosevelt, Christopher Columbus, Oprah Winfrey, Queen Elizabeth I, Mahatma Ghandi, Moses, Mr. Rogers, Attila the Hun, Lee Iacocca, Bill Gates, Mother Theresa, Fidel Castro

1. Which Alpha Leader would be the most effective *communicator* in your workplace? _____

2. Which Alpha Leader would be the most effective at *delegating* in your workplace? _____

3. Which Alpha Leader would be the most effective *problem solver* in your workplace? _____

4. Which Alpha Leader would you *trust in a crisis?* _____

5. From which Alpha Leader *would you prefer to get feedback* regarding your job performance? _____

6. Which Alpha Leader *would you want for your own supervisor?*

   _____

7. Which Alpha Leader most resembles your own style as a manager?

   _____

GAME 2—LOOK, MA, NO HANDS

THE POINT OF THIS GAME

Effective managers **delegate tasks well**. This means they can strike a balance between micromanaging (overseeing every detail of their staff's work) and undermanaging (assigning tasks and then cutting people loose without providing sufficient guidance or support). This entertaining game aptly demonstrates different management styles.

TIME NEEDED

25 minutes

MATERIALS NEEDED

- A large suitcase with a variety of items and clothes to be packed in it. Some things you might include: a suit, a dress, a hairdryer, a small iron, tissue paper, plastic bags, toiletries, shoes, socks, pantyhose, pajamas, bathrobe, and other sundry items someone might use on a trip. (*Note:* Be sure to add a couple of gag items, like Valentine underwear, a teddy bear, bunny slippers, binoculars, etc.)
- Have all the items to be packed and the suitcase laid out on a table at the front of the room.
- Three Expert Packer cards (see handout)

A SUGGESTED FUNNY INTRODUCTION

[Use these show-of-hands questions to get six volunteers:]

"How many have had to sit on a suitcase to get it to shut? You? Thank you. Anyone had luggage-on-wheels that constantly tipped over as you ran for the plane? You and you? Okay! Anyone ever successfully sneak oversized luggage through as carry-on? You, you, and you? Impressive—that's not easy to do. Who's ever walked away with someone else's suitcase by mistake? You? Whoa, that's a drag. ..."

HOW TO PLAY THIS GAME

ROUND 1:

1. Divide your six volunteers into pairs. Tell the pairs they have 30 seconds to determine who has the most dental fillings; this will be Person A, the other Person B. Give Persons A their description cards to read.

2. Inform the pairs that Persons A are famous globe-trotters who lecture to the world, via TV satellite, on "How to Pack for Intercontinental Travel." The only snag: Persons A have no arms. For years now they have relied on their trusted assistants, Persons B, to hide this fact from their cable TV public—in short, to act as the missing appendages.

3. Practice a little: Persons A now stand facing the audience, clasping their hands behind their backs, elbows slightly bent. Persons B stand behind them and thrust their arms through the gap between elbows and ribcage, effectively creating false arms for Persons A.

4. Turn to your learners and say: "We are most fortunate to have with us today three of the most famous packing experts in the world: Dr. Samsonite, Dr. Vuittan, and Dr. Itwas-Onsale. Doctors, please say hello to our audience. [Your volunteers will almost certainly take the cue: Persons A will say, "Hello," while Persons B will wave or some such. If this is at all confusing for them, simply ask a couple of interview-type questions, such as "Where are you from, Doctor?" to let them get the hang of it.]

5. Now begin the game. Say: "Each of these illustrious experts will show us a special method and style of packing. All of these radical, yet effective, methods let the packer to do the job in less than 3 minutes. Dr. Samsonite will demonstrate his[her] method first, using all the materials displayed on the table. Let us welcome Dr. Samsonite!" (Lead applause.)

6. The first pair now comes to stand behind the table with the luggage, facing the audience. Person A begins the lecture, using the delegation style described on his or her card.

7. After 3 minutes, or when all the items have been packed, call time and ask the following:

   - What did you observe about Dr. Samsonite's communication style in this demo?

   - To Person B: What did you observe about how your partner communicated with you? How did you feel about it? What worked or didn't work?

   - To Person A: What was it like to be you in this demo? Was this different from or similar to your communication style in real life?

   - If Person A was really a manager instead of a luggage expert, what would this manager's theories and beliefs about delegation probably be?

ROUND 2:

1. Ask the next pair, with Dr. Vuittan as the expert, to go to the front of the room.

2. Once again, after 3 minutes, or when all the items have been packed, call time and again ask the debriefing questions above.

ROUND 3:

1. Call the third pair, with Dr. Itwas-Onsale, to the front of the room.

2. Call time after 3 minutes, or when all the items have been packed. Lead applause for all three experts, and invite them to return to their seats.

DEBRIEFING QUESTIONS

- What happened in the last demo that was different from the previous ones?
- What did this expert do that was effective?
- What style of delegation would you say the last expert illustrated?
- In what situations might each of these three styles of delegation work best? For example, is there a situation when a micromanaging style would be the most effective? [Answer: When the need for precision and the risks for failure are high, for example, instructing a new surgeon during an operation.]
- In this game, the expert was literally using another person's hands. How does delegation in real life model this?
- What might be the pitfalls of perceiving and using employees simply as another pair of hands?

  [Some possible answers: Humans need to feel they have input and control over their jobs. Relegating individuals to simply perform someone else's vision can adversely impact their commitment and creativity. People feel they're not trusted and become irritated and demotivated; stop taking responsibility for their work; lose the confidence to make decisions on their own. And let's not forget, it's exhausting for the manager!]

- This demo also illustrated a manager who believes employees will learn by themselves, through experience. What are some problems with undermanaging? [Possible answers: This manager usually delegates too much to employees; doesn't provide adequate feedback so the staff knows they're on the right track; ends up having to fix a lot of mistakes and put out a lot of fires.]
- How do you determine what is appropriate to delegate in real life?
- How do you determine what a person is ready for?
- How might you change or challenge your own style of delegation based on this activity?

TIPS ON MAKING THIS GAME WORK WELL

You may want to meet with Persons A after giving them their description cards. Advise them that during the demonstration they should say: "Now *I'll* do this or that" instead of "Now *we'll*. ..." It's just funnier.

Encourage Persons A to justify their partners' actions. ("I see I'm putting my socks in my arm sleeves. Well, it's important to keep your socks warm.") This will get huge laughs of delight, while still making the point.

If it's too inconvenient to bring a suitcase full of stuff to your workshop, you can ask the experts to demonstrate another task, such as making a peanut butter sandwich. Change the names of your experts to match the new task.

OTHER TOPICS THIS GAME TEACHES

- Conflict and Negotiation
- Communication Skills

EXPERT PACKER CARDS

HANDOUT

Distribute one card to each volunteer playing the Expert Packers.

Expert 1: You play Dr. Samsonite, a world-famous packing expert demonstrating your unique packing method to the class. During this activity you will have an assistant who will actually do the packing for you. You are to micromanage your "hands." Give specific and detailed instructions for every step. ("First I'm going to pick up this blouse at the collar. Now I'll hold onto the right shoulder.") Don't allow your assistant to make any independent decisions.

Expert 2: You play Dr. Vuittan, a world-famous packing expert demonstrating your unique packing method to the class. During this activity, you will have an assistant who will actually do the packing for you. Let your assistant do whatever he or she wants and simply state what's happening without offering any future direction. For example: "I am putting the socks into this sleeve. Now I'm sticking my toothbrush into my shoes." You should justify each action to the class ("That's the way my mother taught me"), but you should not offer any specific directions or feedback.

Expert 3: You play Dr. Itwas-Onsale, a world-famous packing expert demonstrating your unique packing method to the class. During this activity, you will have an assistant who will actually do the packing for you. Coach your "hands" through the process, first describing what needs to be done ("I will start by folding the pants") and then verbally guiding your assistant through the packing. Let your assistant try out techniques, and give corrective feedback when needed. "I think this shoe would go better at the lower corner."

GAME 3—CONFUCIUS SAYS

THE POINT OF THIS GAME

This game can be played as an **icebreaker** or as a **review game**. As an ice-breaker, the game intro-duces the workshop goals and content to the learners while setting a playful tone for participa-tory learning. As a review game, Confucius Says reinforces the learning points made throughout the day. This game also demonstrates the principle of random access described in Chapter 2.

TIME NEEDED

10 minutes, depending on the number of learners

MATERIALS NEEDED

- Two Chinese fortune cookies for each learner (*Note:* These can be bought at many supermarkets or Asian food stores.)
- A container labeled Venerable Management Secrets to hold the cookies
- Blank flip chart paper
- Goals or Agenda for the day on flip chart paper or Power Point
- Small prizes (optional)

A SUGGESTED FUNNY INTRODUCTION

"Anyone ever see someone who opens up a fortune cookie *and reads it out to the whole table* like it's a message from some

Higher Being? Anybody ever done it yourself? [Note: If anyone raises a hand, hasten to say: "So have I! It's weird. What are we thinking?"] I mean, we all know these things are probably typed out right in the bakery—probably by the baker during cigarette breaks. And here we are, all over America, sitting in Chinese restaurants going, 'Ooooh, listen to *mine*. …!'

"When people do that, sometimes I mess with them a little. Once a gal said, "Oooh, listen to *mine*: 'Always aim your arrow at the stars. Even if it falls short—'" and I said, "It could still hit Uranus!"

"I don't know, was that rude of me?

"Anyhow, we are now going to make up our own fortune cookie messages. And at the end of the day, the most *profound* message and the *funniest* message will each win a *fabulous prize*! So, let's go!"

HOW TO PLAY AS AN ICEBREAKER

1. Invite each learner to take one fortune cookie from the special container labeled Venerable Management Secrets and read the message.

2. Ask each learner to think of some way to relate this message to a management principle that might be discussed during today's workshop.

3. Ask learners to introduce themselves, read their fortunes aloud, and share the connection to good management principles.

4. Write down each principle on flip chart paper.

5. When all the principles have been shared, go through the list and underline the principles that will be discussed or examined in this workshop. Graciously acknowledge that those not covered are such venerable secrets that even *you*, the workshop leader, had never heard of them before. Lead applause.

6. Award the most important and the most creative connections with small prizes. Tell your learners you look forward to

more of this impressive creative thinking throughout the workshop.

7. Share your prepared workshop goals with the group and launch into the workshop.

HOW TO PLAY AS A REVIEW

1. At the end of the day, invite each learner to choose a fortune cookie from the Venerable Management Secrets container. Lead them in ceremoniously breaking open their cookies and munching on them.

2. Ask some funny show-of-hands questions to find 5 to 10 volunteers. (Examples: "How many have ever felt a surge of anti-establishment pride when you sneaked 12 items through the 9-item supermarket express lane?" "How many have successfully defended 'your' clothes drier from someone who wanted to use it at the laundromat?" "How many have ever gone to the store for milk and come back with a waffle iron, batteries, potato chips, bathroom stick-ons, a calendar, and bean dip—but forgot the milk?")

3. Have the volunteers read their fortunes aloud and ask the entire group to brainstorm some ways to relate each fortune to a principle that was discussed during the day. (*Note:* You can also ask each learner to relate his or her fortune cookie to a principle offered in the round that took place during the icebreaker, which may or may not have been discussed during the day.)

4. Award the most *important to remember* and the most *creative* connections with small prizes.

TIPS ON MAKING THESE GAMES WORK WELL

When giving awards, it is quicker for you to decide on the winners than to put it to a vote. We recommend mentally noting the really good fortunes as they come up throughout, so that you can announce your winners quickly.

Another good way to choose winners is to pay attention to the responses of your learners to the fortunes. This strategy will get a higher level of buy-in from the group. Still, you may sometimes want to forsake it in favor of reinforcing an unexciting but important principle you want learners to remember.

That being said, *any fortunes that get a strong response from your learners should at least be acknowledged sometime during the day.* Jotting down the gist of these messages so that you can paraphrase them later will help. If any of the fortunes get laughs, be *sure* to quote those again at the end of the day! This is a real crowd-pleaser: Even though your learners have already heard them once before, for some reason they will howl the second time around. This is extremely gratifying to the learners who wrote them, and it's a great way for you to focus out (see Chapter 1)—in short, it's worth the effort in terms of the goodwill it generates.

OTHER TOPICS THIS GAME TEACHES

You can easily adapt this game to introduce or review any workshop topic.

GAME 4—MADISON AVENUE TALENT AGENTS

THE POINT OF THIS GAME

Effective managers are careful to **give their employees appropriate praise and positive feedback**. Many managers focus mostly on what employees are doing *wrong*. Often this is because the manager assumes the employees "know when they've done well, and don't need me to cuddle them." Keirsey and Bates* tell us: "Whatever our temperaments, we are all social creatures, and so want to please the boss." *This means that we as managers must make a point of acknowledging our staff members' contributions and efforts.* In this game, your learners get to practice reframing observations to look for the positive, and giving authentic praise.

TIME NEEDED

40 minutes

MATERIALS NEEDED

Talents Worksheet for half the group (see handout)

A SUGGESTED FUNNY INTRODUCTION

"How many think your boss *raves* about you during high-level management meetings? [Look surprised when few or no hands go up.] *No?* Gee ... you mean there are managers out there who don't appreciate their staff's contributions?**

---

*David Keirsey and Marilyn Bates, *Please Understand Me* (Gnosology Books, Ltd., 1984), a very useful and readable manual on applying the Myers-Briggs Type Indicator.

**This is hardly a screamingly funny line, but it *will* get laughs. That's because it touches a very strong emotional chord within most workers today, who, when asked to list the things they would like *more* of in the workplace, generally choose appreciation above money! This, of course, is the key issue of this game.

"Oh, yeah ... I had a boss like that once. One time he gave me such a bad job evaluation that I not only didn't get my raise, I had to *return* the salary I'd made over the last three months! Everyone hated this guy. In fact, we all secretly learned to give CPR *in reverse,* just in case. ...*

"Seriously, research has shown that one of the best ways to win the Most Hated Manager Award is to undermine or ignore your staff members' contributions. The fact is, even the most dedicated, self-directed human beings *do better work when they receive expressions of approval from their leaders.*

"So what do you say—want to get better at bringing out the best in your staff? I thought you would. ... Let's go!"

HOW TO PLAY THIS GAME

1. Create a "fishbowl" by dividing your learners into two equal groups and having them sit in two concentric circles.

2. Assign learners from the outer circle to learners in the inner circle, so that each person is matched up.

3. Give people on the outer circle the Talents Worksheets, and have them read the directions.

4. Now tell the people in the inner circle:

   "You are members of a think tank in a creative, savvy ad agency. The head of your agency has given you the assignment to create a product that will somehow make the world a better place. Your product can be of any size, price, or use. Your job as a group is to come up with 1) the product, 2) a snappy name for it, and 3) the ad jingle.

   "As creative people, each of you naturally retains an agent, who makes a hefty commission by knowing your strengths and constantly communicating them to other firms who may want to steal you from your present employer at a higher

---

*These jokes come from Gene and Linda Perret's book of business-related humor, *Funny Business,* Prentice Hall, Inc., 1990.

salary. But that's *their* job. Right now, *yours* is to come up with this brilliant ad campaign. You have 20 minutes. Go!"

5. After the think tank has formulated its ad campaign (which, believe us, will be one laughter-filled exercise—learners never fail to come up with weird products and downright hilarious jingles), lead the applause.

6. Reconvene the group into one large circle, with the Talent Agents and Creatives sitting side by side. Ask the Talent Agents to brag about their clients' talents for 3 minutes. (*Note:* Agents should describe their clients as if they were speaking to avaricious competitors.)

DEBRIEFING QUESTIONS

To those in the inner circle:

- Was your participation in the inner circle typical of how you work in teams at your worksite? If so, how? If not, how?

- What was it like to hear your Agent's observations of you? Did any of them take you by surprise?

   To those in the outer circle:

- What was it like to concentrate only on someone's strengths? Did you have any trouble reframing the person's behavior in positive terms?

   To everyone:

- **KEY POINT:** Shinichi Suzuki amazed the world by showing us that three-year-olds can play Mozart. It turns out he accomplishes his miracle largely by commenting *only* on the things these tiny children do *right*! Suzuki believes that human beings naturally seek perfection—that it is not enough to master *parts* of our jobs, but the *whole* of them—and that leaders play a vital role in encouraging this drive to mastery. His philosophy: Whatever tasks a leader does *not* praise become top priority for the follower to improve upon. How might you do your job differently if *your* supervisor behaved like a Talent Agent for you, focusing only on your strengths? How would this affect 1) your relationship with them, and 2) your belief in your own competence?

- What would *you* have to do differently to focus on your employees' strengths?

- How do you think your employees might respond if you were to go out of your way to give them positive feedback on a regular basis?

- What internal misgivings might you have to overcome in order to do this? [Probable answer: I can't give only positive feedback. Sometimes you *have* to point out errors to ensure they don't happen again. Your response: True—our staff are not playing the piano or violin, but performing tasks in which errors can be costly or even catastrophic. Have the group discuss what a good praise-to-criticism ratio might be for their staff. Another possible answer: I don't have *time* to keep "stopping and stroking"—I'll never get anything done! Your response: Many times positive feedback is simply saying, "Nice work!" as you walk past an employee's desk. Who doesn't have time for that? Another possible answer: Won't I sound *phony* if I'm constantly saying, "Nice work, nice work, nice work"? Your response: Only if you say it when they're doing lousy work!]

OTHER TOPICS THIS GAME TEACHES

Team Building

TALENT AGENT WORKSHEET

Directions: You are a Madison Avenue Talent Agent, and your partner is your client. Your job is to catalogue your client's gifts and abilities so you can sell your client to headhunters. During this activity you will observe your client closely and focus on everything your client does. In fact, try to interpret *everything* your client does in a positive light. For example, if your client doesn't say a word, frame her or him as "thoughtful." Conversely, if your client dominates the group, then call him or her a "natural leader." Here are some questions to consider in defining your client's strengths:

What did your client do or say to help the group come to a decision?

What was spectacular about how your client communicated with the other team members?

What were your client's best ideas?

Describe your client's impressive intellectual abilities.

Why should the other talent scouts envy you for having this client?

GAME 5—THE HIRING GAME

THE POINT OF THIS GAME

Good managers find competent, cooperative employees by using **strong interviewing techniques.** They ask questions more penetrating than the usual, "Where did you work before?" When listening to answers, they read between the lines. They note the nonverbal messages (especially *incongruent* ones). They listen as much to what isn't said as to what is. This game helps your learners develop and test potential interviewing questions as well as practice their listening and assessing skills.

TIME NEEDED

30–40 minutes

MATERIALS NEEDED

- Flip chart paper and markers for 4 small groups
- Flip chart with the following question categories written on it: Tasks, Relationships, Emotional Intelligence, Values and Attitudes
- An Interview Questions sheet (see handout)
- Three Role Description cards (see page handout)
- Three 3 x 5-inch cards with large, black numbers (1, 2, and 3) printed on them
- Preparation: Set up four stools or chairs at the front of the room. They should be in a roughly chevron formation, with three on the left and one on the right.

A SUGGESTED FUNNY INTRODUCTION

"Every manager prays nightly for one thing: that the employees they hire won't turn out to be either bumbling incompetents or sociopaths! Agreed? [Show of hands. Many of your attendees will probably nod energetically and laugh.] Yes. We *crave* assistants we can give a job to, and know it will be done right the first time. We *yearn* for workers who don't come up to us eight times a day with questions and problems. And heaven knows, we *hunger* for a staff that *get along*! Right? [Show of hands; lots of nods, laughs.]

"In short, we hope the people we hire will make our load lighter, not heavier.

"Has anyone here ever hired someone who was a dream in the job interview ... and a *nightmare* on the job? [Allow one or two learners to share their Jeckyll-and-Hyde stories. If no one has had this experience—which is unlikely, since it's amazingly common—be ready with a story of your own. This will get laughs, not to mention some groans, as it strikes that priceless emotional chord, powerfully reinforcing the value of good interviewing techniques.]

"Yep. Hiring someone is like getting married—you need to look *way* beyond the pretty face! Let's learn how to do this. ..."

HOW TO PLAY THIS GAME

1. You may want to begin this game with an explanation and description of in-depth and behavior-based interviewing.

2. Divide the learners into four teams. Assign each team a Question Category. Each team will brainstorm three to five interviewing questions from the assigned category.

Question Categories

- Task Questions (Example: What's the best thing to do when a decision needs to be made, but there are no guidelines from above?)

- Relationship Questions (Example: What kind of people *don't* you get along with?)
- Emotional Intelligence Questions (Example: How do you respond when your team disagrees with your idea?)
- Values and Attitudes Questions (Example: Is honesty *always* the best policy? If not, then what?)

3. Give the teams 5 minutes to brainstorm questions and to record their questions on the flip chart paper.

4. Ask each team to choose and circle its favorite two questions. The team can use any criteria to choose these questions (hardest to answer, most likely to reveal a weakness, most unusual question).

5. Ask each team to post the flip charts and read aloud the questions.

6. Get four volunteers. (Tip: You may want to use the learners who raised their hands about the Jeckyll-and-Hyde question in your introduction. For other fun ways to find willing volunteers, see Game 3 in this chapter or Game 1 in Chapter 10.)

7. Three of the volunteers will play job applicants, and the fourth will be the interviewer. Hand the applicants their Role Description cards, and ask them to sit down on their three stools and read them silently. (*Note:* make a point of saying, "Please—do *not* laugh or in any other way give away your role!" This will help ensure your "surprise guest" doesn't inadvertently reveal his or her identity, while it will heighten curiosity among the other learners.)

8. Meanwhile, have the interviewer take the single stool. Explain that you have narrowed down scores of job applicants to the best three. The interviewer will now have 7 minutes to interview the three top prospects. Have the interviewer quickly look over the posted questions that were just brainstormed by the teams. The interviewer can use any particularly useful questions from that list and may make up others on the spot.

9. Now turn to the class and say:

"Welcome, ladies and gentlemen, to ... *The Hiring Game!* Yes, that's right, it's time for that fun-filled show where our intelligent but wary manager tries to decide which of three *alluring* competitors is not just a 'pretty face,' but will actually be able to *do the job*—and do it without being a *royal pain in the neck!*

"Yes, this is the moment of truth ... when a manager makes a decision that will affect not only the department's *productivity,* but its *mental health*—and maybe even its future legal costs!

"Our manager will have to look beyond the glib words and sweet smiles, and see the hidden truth: Is each applicant really the godsend he or she *appears* to be ... or is there some hidden, fatal flaw that the manager—and his or her staff—will have to live with for years to come? Which applicant will today's manager choose? Let's find out. ..."

10. Your interviewer now gets to ask the applicants, one at a time, any of the posted questions (or any other in-depth questions). At the end of 7 minutes, call time, and have the manager choose the person he or she wants to hire.

11. Now have the rest of the class vote on whomever *they* would hire. A simple show of hands will do; count the votes and jot down which applicant comes in first, second, and third. Give the "1" card to the class's first choice, the "2" to the second choice, and the "3" to the third. Have the applicants hold up their cards in view of the class.

12. Invite the applicants now to step forward, one by one, and read their Role Description card identities. (One way to do this is for #3 to come forward first, followed by #2, and then #1. A tip: Whenever possible, it's *very* effective to have the ax-murderer go last. And, of course, expect an explosion of laughter if this is the person who got hired!)

13. Thank all your contestants, lead the applause, and have them sit down.

DEBRIEFING QUESTIONS

- Which questions were the most effective in revealing the applicants' strengths?
- Which questions were the most effective in revealing the applicants' weaknesses?
- How well did your team's favorite questions work in this situation? What makes an interview question effective or not effective in real life?
- What questions do you wish had been asked?
- How did the applicants in this activity *hide* or reframe their weaknesses? How do job candidates do this in real life? What questions could you ask to reveal a more accurate picture?

TIPS ON MAKING THIS GAME WORK WELL

It is fun to have game show music playing as you do the introduction in Step 9. Tapes of this (and other legally usable music) are available.* You can use a portable tape or CD player for this. Be sure to have the tape cued to the music, so that it comes on immediately when you press the Play button. And try fading the volume out at the end of your introduction, rather than just hitting the Stop button.

*At the time of this writing, the only source we have found that offers fun, copyright-free taped music is Trainer's Warehouse. For a catalogue of their products, you can call 1-800-299-3770, or visit their website at www.trainerswarehouse.com.

APPLICANT 1—SAM (OR SALLY) LANDFILL

You have all the skills needed for this job and then some. This is because you are a perfectionist—whatever you do, you always do extraordinarily well.

Because of your outstanding performance at your previous company, in which you broke all records for both output and quality, you were named Employee of the Year. In fact, the only reason you left that job is that you needed better opportunities for advancement: Your boss was well-liked and in good health, so there was little chance of your getting *her* job anytime soon. Also, you didn't have the best relationship with your peers, who seemed to find you an unapproachable "cold fish."

Please answer the interview questions as if you were really this person—that is, try to put yourself in the best light without lying. For instance, you probably won't want to mention that you were after your old boss's job, as this might make the new boss nervous. And you will probably downplay—or skip altogether—the subject of colleague relations. You know you brought exceptional ability to your last job; your coworkers' feelings were simply a secondary concern with you. And that's how it should be. After all, we're not at work to win popularity contests. Still and all, it's probably wisest to keep answers to any "people skills" questions brief and positive.

APPLICANT 2—ED (OR EDNA) CASSEROLE

You are fresh out of a good college, with state-of-the-art skills in the job you now seek. You have no paid experience in this industry, but you have lots of experience in interning, as well as volunteering in college groups, political campaigns, charities, and the like. You have a folder full of enthusiastic references from supervisors in these areas. More than that, you have sincere enthusiasm for this job, and are willing to be molded! In addition, you get along with all types of people, and are always extremely well-liked wherever you work.

Please answer the interview questions as you yourself would in a real-life job interview situation. Just throw in the above facts here and there as appropriate. A winning tip: Emphasize 1) how excited you are about this particular organization, and 2) how easy you find most people to get along with. Above all, be sincere! (Fake it if you have to.)

APPLICANT 3—CHARLES (OR CHARLOTTE) CURBFEELER

You have solid work experience in some of the top firms in this industry. You are also a quick study, so the few skills you *don't* have you will pick up fast! For example, when your last company underwent a rapid expansion, you were put in charge of a new department and within four months increased the return on investment by 20 percent. You have sterling references and your colleagues have always liked you and found you pleasant to work with.

There's just one little problem: You are an ax-murderer. But you only dispatch strangers—never customers or colleagues. Well, almost never. Oh, dear.

Please answer the interview questions as you would if you were really this person: Try to put yourself in the best light, coming across as completely normal. Let's face it, someone with your proclivities has to be a good liar. Turn on the charm! Be the dream employee! Bonus points if you get hired.

4

Five Games to Construct Creative, Cooperative Teams

GAME 1—GROUP-MIND STORY

THE POINT OF THIS GAME

An indispensable trait of good teams is cooperation. And an indispensable trait of cooperation is an **outward focus**— the willingness to be as interested in other peoples' thoughts and ideas as you are in your own. We call this Making Your Partner Look Good. Always remember that *in the idea-generation process, you do not think about end results* (see Chapter 2, Five Games to Enhance Creative Thinking and Problem-Solving Skills). The whole team may ultimately decide to go with the idea you brought up in the first place, but during the brainstorming session this isn't the point. Listening to your team members is the point. Put another way, having ideas makes you a good team player; clutching them fiercely to your chest does not.

TIME NEEDED

10–20 minutes, depending on debriefing

MATERIALS NEEDED

None

A SUGGESTED FUNNY INTRODUCTION

"How many of you can make up a whole story on the spot? [Show of hands.] Hmmm. How many can make up one paragraph of a story on the spot? [Show of hands.] Okay. How many can come up with one word on the spot? [Show of hands.] All *right*! Looks like we can play this game!"

HOW TO PLAY THIS GAME

1. Tell the group you are all going to make up a story together, with each member contributing only one word at a time. The hitch: Each member must choose words that are as *interesting* and *original* as possible.

2. Pick a volunteer from the group to demonstrate. You and the volunteer will create a story beginning with "Once upon a time …" Begin by saying: "Once" and point to the volunteer to say the next word (*upon*). Continue alternating words until you have reached a natural ending. Close the story with the ending phrase: "The moral of this story is …" with you and the volunteer alternating words to come up with a profound ending.

3. Start the whole group off. You might begin with a word like, "Yesterday …" or stick with the "Once upon a time" opening. Point to Person 2, who says something like, "I …" Point to Person 3: "Killed …" Person 4: "My …" Person 5: "Mother." Person 6: "I …" Person 7: "Ate …" Person 8: "Custard." Continue till it feels as if the story has run its course.

4. Now start a new story, with a new instruction: This time the words must:

    a. Be as *unoriginal as possible*. ("Dare to be boring!")

    b. *Make the word of the preceding person work as well as possible*. ("Make you pal look good!")

    Again, continue till it feels as if the story is over.

DEBRIEFING QUESTIONS

- What differences did you notice between the first and the second stories? [See Tips on Making This Game Work Well.]
- If the second story was better, why do you think that was so?
- In this game, did anyone have the experience of thinking, "No, no, don't say *that*, I meant *this*"? [Show of hands.]
- Did anyone then have the experience of watching the combined intelligence of the group take the new, unexpected idea

and make it work just fine—or even better? [Show of hands.] How did that feel?

- How does all this relate to your work together as a team? What can you do when someone disagrees with or doesn't understand your idea? What have you learned about having faith in combined intelligence—in trusting that the group may be going in a good direction, even if you don't see it yet?

- **KEY POINT:** If everybody focused on making everybody else look good, what would happen in your team?

TIPS ON MAKING THIS GAME WORK WELL

Group-Mind Story can be played with groups of virtually any size and in any type of room setup. Standing in a circle is best, but sitting—theatre or classroom style, even at round tables in a hotel ballroom—is okay. In these setups, move among the learners and point to the person whose turn it is to speak.

Ask learners to speak up, and speak clearly! If they are not facing each other, it may be necessary for you to repeat each word for the others to hear.

Keep the pace fast; this makes the story easier for participants to follow.

Note: Use your training from Chapter 1 (Five Games to Make You a Naturally Funny Trainer) to be ready for whatever happens in this game. The second story almost always works better—has more flow, makes more sense, is easier to tell. Still, no group is 100 percent predictable! At least one of the authors has had the experience of delivering this game to unusually well-educated and literate attendees, who instinctively knew what constitutes a good story. With such attendees, the first and second stories are almost equally well-constructed. Still, subtle differences usually appear, generally in the form of either consistency (logic) within the story, or a sense of enjoyment in creating the story. With such groups, keep an ear open for these two attributes, and be ready to point out such differences as you note them.

OTHER TOPICS THIS GAME TEACHES

- Communication Skills
- Creative Problem Solving

GAME 2—KOMMUNICATION KRAZY KWILT

THE POINT OF THIS GAME

A good team **communicates well.** Good communication involves both sending and receiving information clearly. We are good receivers—get more mistake-free messages—if we keep our attention *focused outward* (see Group-Mind Story). We are good senders if we make a habit of *checking in,* to ensure our message was clear.

TIME NEEDED

15–20 minutes

MATERIALS NEEDED

None

A SUGGESTED FUNNY INTRODUCTION

"And now for a game I know you're going to love. And I want to assure you right now: your brains will only be sore for a couple of days. Okay, please stand up now and form a circle. ..."

HOW TO PLAY THIS GAME

1. Start things off by pointing to anyone in the circle and saying, "You!" (Keep pointing.) That person puts a hand on his or her head to signify "taken," then points to someone else, saying, "You!" That person puts a hand on his or her head, points

to another person, and says, "You." Keep going until the last person points to, well, *you*. Put a hand on your own head.

2. Now everyone is pointing to someone else. Each of you make a mental note of who your Sender and Receiver are, then lower both hands.

3. Begin again: Each person, in turn, says, "You," this time *making eye contact only* with the Receiver. Do this three or four more times, faster and faster, till the group has the pattern firmly established ("He sends to *me*, I send to *her*").

4. Now start a completely new pattern. Tell everyone you're going to do vegetables this time, then point to a new Receiver (anyone but the person you pointed to the first time) and say something like, "Cauliflower!" The person puts a hand on his or her head, points to someone new, and says, maybe, "Spinach!" Continue till the last person sends a vegetable to you. Run through your veggie pattern three or four times till it is firmly established.

5. Switch back to the "You" pattern. Can everyone remember the Receiver from the first time? Run through it a couple of times. Then switch to the Veggie pattern. Run through that. Keep switching back and forth until the group can alternate with ease.

6. Now comes the really fun part: Look at your first Receiver and say, "You," then immediately turn to your second one and say, "Cauliflower!" The two patterns are now going on simultaneously. The group knows it has succeeded when you, the leader, receive both a "You" and a vegetable back again. Lead a cheer when this happens.

Note: Debrief as necessary to keep the game going. For example, if the group keeps losing patterns, suggest that they speak more loudly and clearly; make stronger eye contact; and most important *keep attention on their Receivers after sending them the word, to ensure they got it and passed it on!* (Remember, that's the Sender's job.)

DEBRIEFING QUESTIONS

- What made it hard to keep all the patterns in play at once?
- What can we do to be better Receivers in this game? How can we be better Senders?
- How easy was it to pay close attention to both your Sender *and* your Receiver at the same time? [Note: Answers typically include some variation of: "Ghaaaaaah!" Make sympathetic sounds.]
- What's required to make this balancing act a little easier? [Note: Someone will often say, "Schizophrenia!" Don't forget to laugh at the joke, no matter how many times you hear it.] Okay, good. What else is required?
- Obviously you had to communicate at warp capacity for this game; but how do you think these skills could be modified and adapted to your daily communications with each other?

TIPS ON MAKING THIS GAME WORK WELL

The ideal size of a circle is 8 to 15 people. If you have more learners than this, just form a small group and demonstrate the game to the class at large. Then create as many circles as needed, appoint a leader for each, and set them loose! Move about, monitoring each circle.

Pick any kinds of categories you please—cars, movie stars, animals, authors, countries; the list is endless.

Most groups can manage at least three patterns at one time, and some four or five. Bear in mind, however, that different groups learn patterns at very different speeds. It is important to pace this game so that the challenge is commensurate with the group's ability; don't let faster groups get bored or slower ones get discouraged.

With superfast groups, you might add an extra (and *superfun*) element to the game: In the "You" pattern, have each Sender walk over and take the place of the Receiver, who must then go and take the place of their Receiver, and so on. Do this while three or four patterns are going on simultaneously. Believe us, this'll keep their attention!

It can also be fun not to announce new categories. Instead just launch into one—"My Three Sons!"—and see what happens. The person you point to will usually catch on at once—"The Brady Bunch!"—and the group will be on its way. But sometimes a lovely moment happens: Doni remembers one group in which the first word was Poe (as in Edgar Allen). The second person looked perplexed for an instant, then shrugged and said, "Rich?" The group dissolved into laughter—then got bonus points for immediately taking up the new category: financially secure, comfortable, just scraping by, liquid, etc. Very nice indeed.

OTHER TOPICS THIS GAME TEACHES

- Management Skills
- IceBreaker

GAME 3—PUSHY PARTNERS

THE POINT OF THIS GAME

A good team **accepts and knows how to handle conflict**. Like stress, conflict is inevitable; like stress, it can also be both positive and negative. Positive dynamics of conflict include increased energy and attention. Negative ones include resistance and defensiveness. This quick game illustrates typical negative dynamics of conflict. (*Note:* The game can also beautifully illustrate concepts such as Kurt Lewin's Force Field theory, which explores the impact of enabling and restraining forces; or Chris Argyris's work on double-loop learning and defensive behavior.) The debriefing discussion can also serve as an introduction to the importance of question-asking to defuse conflict. (See Tips on Making This Game Work Well.)

TIME NEEDED

5 minutes or more, depending on extent of debriefing

MATERIALS NEEDED

Watch with timer

A SUGGESTED FUNNY INTRODUCTION

We find it best to simply ask your learners to stand up and play this game. The lack of context builds curiosity, which lasts throughout the simple activity. It inspires a burst of bewildered

83

laughter afterward when, without comment, you politely ask them to sit back down. The debriefing session is that much more intriguing for the suspense.

HOW TO PLAY THIS GAME

1. Pair up the learners and have them stand facing each other. Ask them to raise their hands and place their palms against their partners'.

2. When you call "Go," they must push against their partners' hands. Encourage them throughout: "Keep pushing. Push! Just a few seconds longer. That's it, push! Keep on pushing."

3. After 30 seconds to a minute, call time, thank everyone, and ask them to sit back down. (*Note:* Again, they will give you quizzical stares or laughs. Just smile back pleasantly.)

DEBRIEFING QUESTIONS

- When you pushed against your partner's hands, *what did your partner need to do in order to maintain equilibrium?* [Answer: Push back.]

- If you pushed harder, *what did your partner have to do in response?* [Answer: Push back harder.]

- Think about responding to someone with a different outlook, idea, or opinion from your own. How could you verbally "push" in those situations, making the other person want to push back harder against *you?* [Suggested answer: Start off by contradicting the person's idea.]

- What are some ways you could respond to an opinion you disagree with that *wouldn't* result in the other person feeling pushed against? [**KEY POINT:** Start off with clarifying, neutral *questions*, rather than *statements* opposing the position.]

- Are there any additional benefits to asking questions about an opinion or idea you don't immediately agree with?

TIPS ON MAKING THIS GAME WORK WELL

You may want to enhance the game's point with a cold versus hot water metaphor. Say, "When you drop an egg into hot water, it hardens. When you drop it into cold water, it remains soft. Argumentative statements are like hot water: They tend to make people firm up in resolve to have things their way. Questions let your partner stay cool and soft—and ultimately more open to hearing and considering *your* ideas later on."

Note: Some people are uncomfortable about touching other people due to cultural or personality preferences. As always, give your learners the option not to participate in this game if it makes them uncomfortable. They will learn as much from watching and listening to the debriefing as from taking part in the activity.

OTHER TOPICS THIS GAME TEACHES

- Conflict and Negotiation
- Reducing Workplace Negativity
- Communication Skills
- Dealing with Difficult People
- Customer Service

GAME 4—ONE LITTLE WORD

THE POINT OF THIS GAME

The members of a good team **extend trust and acceptance to each other**. This game illustrates how even a simple thing like word choice can signal trust and acceptance, encouraging a greater degree of cooperative risk-taking during problem-solving sessions. (*Note:* The game is particularly good for groups in which members typically criticize one another's ideas.)

TIME NEEDED

10 minutes

MATERIALS NEEDED

Watch with timer

A SUGGESTED FUNNY INTRODUCTION

"Linus Pauling said, 'The way to get good ideas is to get lots of ideas and throw the bad ones away.'" The problem is, when we're dealing with other people's ideas, we're sometimes a *little* too free with the old garbage disposal switch. And when we get really good at trashing each other's ideas, guess what we end up with? Right: no ideas—and lots of people who wish we were dead!"

HOW TO PLAY THIS GAME

Note: this game is conducted in two rounds.

1. Divide the group into pairs and tell them that the person with the shortest (or least amount of) hair in each pair will be Person A. The pairs will have one minute to plan a vacation together.

2. Round 1: Person A throws out a suggestion. (Example: "Let's go someplace exciting.")

3. Person B responds by saying "Yes, but—" and finishes the sentence. (Example: "*Yes, but* I want to lie on the beach all day.")

4. Person A now says, "Yes, *but*—" and makes another statement. The conversation continues in this vein until the minute is up.

5. Round 2: Person A starts off with the same vacation suggestion. This time, partners respond to each other's suggestions by saying "Yes, *and.*" (Example: "Let's go someplace exciting." "*Yes, and* let's make it someplace we've never seen.") Call time after one minute.

DEBRIEFING QUESTIONS

- Even though you knew this game wasn't real life—that I *told* you to "Yes, but" each other—*how many found your partner was really starting to bug you in Round 1?* [*Note:* this question usually inspires lots of laughter.] Any difference in Round 2?

- How many got further along in your vacation plans the second time? If so, why?

- **KEY POINT:** How can you "Yes, and" someone in real life when you disagree with the person?

- How does the "Yes, and" technique affect power and conflict in dialogue? What would you give up and what would you gain by using this technique when you're in conflict?

- Most important of all, *what kinds of vacations did you come up with?* [*Note:* This question ends the game on a positive, high-energy note, as some of your learners will have planned purely outrageous holidays, which they will love sharing.]

TIPS ON MAKING THIS GAME WORK WELL

You may want to do a short debriefing after Round One, to capitalize on the thoughts and feelings learners are experiencing in that moment. Questions during this debriefing should focus on what the learners are thinking and feeling about their partners and about how well the conversation is going.

OTHER TOPICS THIS GAME TEACHES

- Conflict and Negotiation
- Communication Skills
- Reducing Workplace Negativity

GAME 5—CLASH OF THE TITANS

THE POINT OF THIS GAME

Truly outstanding teams **embrace and celebrate diversity.** They see their members' different styles as enriching, rather than fragmenting. This game lets your learners observe and demonstrate the impact of different personality styles on group functioning.

TIME NEEDED

40 minutes

MATERIALS NEEDED

- Character descriptions for each learner printed on slips of paper (see handouts)
- Name tags or name tents for each role
- Pens and blank sheets of paper for each learner

A SUGGESTED FUNNY INTRODUCTION

"Imagine you are shipwrecked on a gorgeous desert island with a bunch of people you don't know. You've eaten all the exotic, nourishing food you can stuff down; you've thrilled to the dazzling, tropical flora and fauna; you've delighted in the always-perfect weather. There's only one catch: The jerks you were shipwrecked with. One is a blowhard, one's a slacker, one's a wimp ... in fact, every one of them has a major personality flaw. You know you're doomed to spend the rest of your life with these people, and just about now you're starting to wish you'd gone down with the boat!

"Sometimes being on a team can feel like you've been marooned with a bunch of flaming sociopaths. Has anybody ever had this feeling? Or am I the only one? [Show of hands, laughter.]

"In this game, we're going to examine some of the dynamics that contribute to that feeling of alienation—dynamics, by the way, that happen in every group situation—and the behaviors that can help or hinder us in dealing with it."

HOW TO PLAY THIS GAME

1. Divide the learners into groups of five to seven. Give the group the following scenario (we recommend using an impressive, Rod Serling-type voice):

   "The year—1980. You are a team of senior executives in a prestigious, industry-dominating company. The company: 21st-Century Typewriters Unlimited. Each of you has been flown in especially for this emergency meeting. Your mission: Write a memo to your CEO explaining why your company is experiencing slumping typewriter sales. In the next 15 minutes you must draft this memo, describing the reasons for the alarming drop and outlining a marketing plan that will bring sales up. At the end of 15 minutes your CEO's executive secretary will take your memo, ready or not."

2. Give a character role and a name tag or name tent to each person.

3. Ask people to introduce themselves to their group in character, and from then on participate in the discussion in character.

4. After 15 minutes, interrupt the groups and introduce yourself as the CEO's secretary. Ask the groups to give you the memos they have drafted. Thank the groups for their hard work and end the game.

DEBRIEFING QUESTIONS

- How did the mix of personalities parallel your real-life experiences working on teams?

- What did you observe about how your group dealt with its challenge?

- What happens in most teams when personalities clash? How do the original team goals and good intentions change?

- Each character had something *dysfunctional* and something *helpful* to add to the group. What did the character *you* played need in order to be most helpful? What dynamics brought out the worst parts of your character's personality?

OTHER TOPICS THIS GAME TEACHES

- Facilitation Skills
- Management Skills
- Personality Inventory
- Values
- Leadership Skills

CLASH OF THE TITANS CHARACTER DESCRIPTION CARDS

TIFFANY TRUMP OR CHARLES "SUNTAN" GETTY III (THE SOCIALITE)

You flew in on the Concorde for this meeting, and hope to *heaven* it will be over soon because you absolutely *have* to go shopping. Nevertheless, you see the current discussion as a good networking opportunity. You don't see *what* the problem is with the present marketing plan: *you* have always thought the *main* reason sales are falling is that the typewriter keyboards simply aren't conducive to women with long fingernails. (After all, it's women who do most of the typing, right?) Come *on*, people, smell the coffee. Can we move to adjourn now?

DUDLEY OR DEE DEE DORIGHT (THE GOOD SAMARITAN)

You believe we'll have greater success working on this problem if everyone gets along and supports one another's ideas. If you sense any disharmony, you rush right in to make sure we all still like each other. You think typewriter sales are going down because people find the typewriter too complicated and impersonal. You think a new marketing plan should focus on how easy a typewriter is to use.

MARTHA STEWARD OR MIKE MACHIAVELLI (THE KNOW-IT-ALL)

You know you are the natural leader of this group—it's a simple matter of Divine Right. You have vast knowledge and educated opinions on almost every topic. You most certainly know that the reason typewriter sales are falling is that typewriters are so annoyingly noisy. Indeed, you have long advocated that the company develop typewriters with muffled keys, and when they foolishly didn't listen to you, seriously considered starting up your own Quiet Keys Company. Naturally, you have numerous statistics at hand to support your statements.

BARBARA BACK-STABBER OR BARRY BORED (THE PASSIVE-AGGRESSIVE SNIPER)

You are frustrated at having to sit through yet another inane discussion. Anything the group decides is immaterial to you anyway, since you have just accepted a job with a new computer company some guys in a garage developed. Anyway, why should you care about 21st-Century Typewriters after the lousy way they've treated you all these years? Heaven knows they've never given you credit for the host of invaluable contributions you've made to their sorry company.

Come to think of it, it could be fun to offer a few last, *intelligent* solutions to the company's problems. That'll show everybody what they'll be missing when you leave.

PROFESSOR NEO CORTEX (THE THINKER)

You believe that this meeting is alarmingly premature. This group needs more time and more data in order to have any kind of fruitful discussion. In fact, you believe you should have been appointed to chair a research committee to determine why sales are falling. You stolidly maintain that the group cannot move ahead in this discussion until a long-term study with quantifiable data has been completed. You may have to interrupt people frequently to get this point across.

HOLLY OR HAROLD HELPLESS (THE QUIET ONE)

Out of interest, you read the industry journals regularly, but you are rather shy about sharing your opinions (generally you don't talk without encouragement). To you it seems likely that typewriters are on their way out as more Americans are buying these expensive contraptions called personal computers. You think that at this juncture the company might be wise to start manufacturing keyboards instead of typewriters. You will only tell the group this, however, if directly asked. And if challenged, you will immediately back down.

YOU, YOURSELF, AND THOU

Participate in the conversation with your own personality. You are free to support or oppose any of the ideas your teammates suggest.

5

Five Games to Help People Deal with Change

GAME 1—GOODIES AUCTION

THE POINT OF THIS GAME

People who handle change well are willing to **take risks and commit to decisions**. This game allows learners to practice these skills, and to explore fear—including the fear of success! It illustrates how most people feel some trepidation even when making positive or necessary changes. It also shows how our values affect our decisions and the risks we take when we're put "on the spot."

TIME NEEDED

30–40 minutes

MATERIALS NEEDED

- One thousand dollars in play money for each learner (in two $500 bills)
- Ten thousand dollars in play money for banker (in $100 bills)
- Auction sheets for each learner
- Certificates of Ownership for each goody item
- Gavel (optional)
- Pens or pencils

A SUGGESTED FUNNY INTRODUCTION

"How many of you have ever dreamed of winning the lottery? [Show of hands.] What kinds of things would you do? [Let people share some of their fantasies of hitting it big: quitting their jobs immediately (maybe telling off the boss first!); moving to the Virgin Islands; getting a facelift, etc. This two-minute discussion will almost certainly inspire laughs, or at least put learners into a very positive frame of mind!]

"If you've ever imagined winning the lottery, you've probably thought of things like that. Now, how many have *also* thought of the ugly relatives you'll have to dodge, lost friendships, phone calls from strangers in the middle of the night, and whether you'll be bored sitting on the yacht all day? According to psychologists, although we often *say* we want things to change for the better, we also hesitate when faced with the *realities* of change. You've heard of fear of success? People don't really fear success—they fear the negative changes that often go along with success.

"In this game, you'll get to buy elements of a dream job. Like most good things in life, many of these will have a downside. It's up to you to decide how much they're really worth to you."

HOW TO PLAY THIS GAME

1. Distribute the auction sheets (see handouts) and $1,000 each to the learners.

2. Have learners review the goodies listed on their auction sheets and circle the ones they would most like to have in real life. Learners should then budget how much of their play money they're willing to spend to "own" each item. Remind them that they only have $1,000 to spend and that the goodies will be auctioned off in increments of $100. They can divide their allowance among many goodies, or blow the whole wad on one—it's up to them. Note that each item lists the benefits the ownership as well as some downsides.

98

3. When the learners have finished selecting their goodies, introduce yourself as the auctioneer, and give them the rules for the Goodies Auction:

   - All bidding will begin at $100.
   - Learners may only bid in $100 increments.
   - To maintain the sanity of the auctioneer, learners must raise their hands to make their bids. Yelling or screaming of bids will under no circumstances be acknowledged. The auctioneer will point to the successful bidder and confirm the price before asking if there are any higher bids.
   - Learners do not have to abide by their original budgets. They can spontaneously change their plans at any time (until, of course, they've bought an item; then it's theirs, and that money is spent).

4. Begin the auction with a bang from your gavel or some other dramatic opening.

5. Introduce each item in your best auctioneer voice and briefly sell the group on *both its merits and risks*. Ask for a starting bid of $100, and continue selling until the highest bid is reached. Give the proud owner any change that is due and a Certificate of Ownership.

6. When all goodies have been bought, close the auction.

DEBRIEFING QUESTIONS

- What were you thinking and feeling during the auction? What did you observe about others?
- Were there any goodies you really wanted but didn't get? Why not?
- Were there any goodies you were afraid to buy? Why?
- How many people totally abandoned their planned budget once the bidding started? What happened during the auction that made you change your plan?
- In this game, you were only risking play money to get what you want. What do you risk in real life when you are faced

99

with a change, even a positive one? [Possible answers: sense of competence, possible humiliation, loss of status, rejection, money, power, etc.]

- How do the elements of this game (competition with others, limited resources, quick decision making) relate to your real life?

- How does fear of actually getting what we want affect how we approach change and risk? How do we sabotage our own success?

- **KEY POINT:** Look down at the goodies you now own. Imagine for a moment that you really had these items in your life, and that when you left this room, whatever your certificate says you own would magically appear. Ask yourself these questions:

  What would you risk to have these things in real life? How would you decide if it were worth it?

  If you think any of these goodies are worth the risks involved, *what holds you back from having them now?*

  What do you need to feel or know in order to be more open to changes and opportunities?

TIPS ON MAKING THIS GAME WORK WELL

You can reduce the number of goodies depending on the size of your group. What's important is that there is some element of *competition* in the game, so make sure there is not more than a 2 to 1 ratio of items to number of learners.

It might be easier for you to have a second facilitator or a volunteer to play Banker, making change and giving out the certificates during the game.

A variation on this game is to change the rules during play. For example, you can arbitrarily give one or two learners more money during the game for any random reason—modeling real life, where we are not necessarily competing on a level playing field. You can also suddenly announce that two or three goodies are no longer up for auction as they "have been discontinued by the manufacturers." Learners who were counting on buying these items will now have to adjust quickly—again modeling how unpredictable changes in the environment affect our personal goals.

OTHER TOPICS THIS GAME TEACHES

- Values
- Conflict and Negotiation
- Assertiveness

Your Budget	Goody	HANDOUT
	A 200% RAISE IN SALARY. This will, of course, bring you more of the material comforts you want and deserve—even if it also creates the need to find more write-offs that will give you the lowest possible tax burden (*and* the lowest possible chance of being audited). But what's a little accounting hassle? Remember that your family will admire and love you for your prowess as a breadwinner, even as their demands increase for clothes, cars, and other things they know you will provide with your *next* big raise.	
	APPOINTMENT AS PRESIDENT OF YOUR COMPANY'S BOARD OF DIRECTORS Respect, power, challenge—it just doesn't get any better. All those late-night and weekend meetings will be no problem—just watch out for those backroom politics! (Some of those other, empire-building board members can be *vicious*.)	
	REGULAR, PRIVATE MEETINGS WITH YOUR CEO, WHO MUST ACT ON ALL YOUR MANDATES Isn't it about time someone who really understands the nuts and bolts got some say? Your coworkers will love you—*and* the chance to finally have the ear of "one of their own." They'll seek you out constantly. And undoubtedly they'll stand by you if some of their ideas that you passed on don't work out too well!	
	***BIG-TIME* HEALTH BENEFITS** Never fill out another form! Just bring your health card with you on any visit to your MD, dentist, chiropractor or massage therapist, and pay only 20% of cost. (Also, never quit your job—after all, you'd have to be insane to give up all this!)	

Your Budget	Goody
	## SKILLS TRAINING ON DEMAND

The skills in your current position constantly need up-dating. In addition, you never know when you'll be thinking about "moving on." The fact is, ongoing training seems the best route to high employability. On the other hand, sitting through boring seminars and workshops has so far been about as enjoyable as having your fingernails pulled out. Are you sure it's worth it? |
| | ## A COMPANY DAYCARE CENTER, WITH A VERITABLE "MARY POPPINS" STAFF

You get to see your kids on breaks; you'll be informed immediately about illnesses, injuries, and other things. What a load off your mind! Your children may learn to seek love and affection from their daycare staff instead of from *you*. But hey, isn't this exactly what the Royal Family goes through? |
| | ## TWO MONTHS PAID VACATION PER YEAR

No more of those paltry, two-week deals that usually end up as nerve-racking obligatory visits with relatives. This is *real* R&R—a break from the rat race. Take advantage! Do *not* spend it worrying about petty things like 1) returning to a Mount Everest of untouched paperwork on your desk, or, worse still, 2) that everyone's getting along just fine without you. |
| | ## THE FASTEST, MOST USER-FRIENDLY COMPUTER IN YOUR WHOLE COMPANY

Yee-hah! Finally you can get some work done! This will improve your quality of life tremendously. So you can *certainly* afford to be gracious when coworkers beg to log on any time you step away from your desk. |

Your Budget	Goody
	## CUSTOMERS AND COLLEAGUES SO PLEASANT THEY COULD LIVE IN MR. ROGERS' NEIGHBORHOOD Could there possibly be a downside to this? Heaven knows, we can't think of one. ...
	## A BOSS SO PLEASANT S/HE *TAUGHT* MR. ROGERS HOW TO BE NICE Ditto.
	## FLEX-TIME Praise heaven! No more fuming in rush-hour gridlock every day. So you have to get up at 4 a.m., or leave work at 8 p.m. Think of the commute hours saved in a year.
	## A COMPANY CAR, *WITH DRIVER*, TO TAKE YOU TO AND FROM WORK Leave road rage to someone else! Instead spend that valuable energy—and commute time—working on company business. (This *is* what your employers expected when they gave you the car, of course.)
	## A GENEROUS CLOTHING ALLOWANCE Nothing's better than knowing you look like a million bucks—unless it's knowing you did it with someone else's money! So what if your bosses and coworkers scrutinize your appearance more critically than they used to—*you* know you have great taste. Bring on the Fashion Police. ...

Your Budget	Goody
	A KEY TO THE COMPANY-OWNED APARTMENT Great for impressing clients, sleeping after 16-hour work days, and plain old midday napping. The fact is, there's *nothing* like executive perks. (And undoubtedly your marriage is strong enough so that your spouse won't wonder what other opportunities that apartment affords you. …)
	TELECOMMUTING Working from home is pure bliss. Get up and stretch when you wish; roam to your well-stocked refrigerator at will; play any music you like from your own personal CD collection. There is certainly no danger of *distractions*—you can easily turn off *Oprah* when the work at hand needs your attention!
	YOUR OWN CORNER OFFICE WITH WINDOWS, FOUR WALLS, AND A LOCKED DOOR Ah, privacy! It's great to be out of the general work area, with its chatter and gossip. Even if it's *you* they sometimes talk about now that you're "removed," who cares? You can rely on the head honchos of your organization to know any petty backbiting is untrue.
	A GOURMET LUNCH, COOKED TO YOUR ORDER AND BROUGHT TO YOU EVERY DAY Enough cafeteria fare! Some of us just *appreciate* fine food. No doubt about it, this goody will add significantly to your quality of life at work. (You need only take the appropriate steps to ward off the weight gain that could possibly accompany it.)

Your Budget	Goody
	## YOUR OWN EXECUTIVE BATHROOM WITH JACUZZI Okay, so most execs seldom have time to use these suckers—you know *you* will. (And if not, you can at least brag that you have one. That should increase your popularity tremendously!)
	## RELOCATION TO THE CITY OF YOUR CHOICE New York, Paris, Hong Kong, the Cayman Islands—now's your chance to live out your dreams! Be ready to leave family and friends behind (you'll certainly see them again, *often,* over the years). For now, get ready to experience something many people only imagine. Seek out brave, new worlds, go where no one has gone before! The Force be with you. ...
	## YOUR OWN PARKING SPOT RIGHT NEXT TO YOUR OFFICE No more lateness, no more of that unpleasant cardio-vascular exercise walking from your car to the building entrance—and *everyone* will know who you are! Some of your coworkers are a little envious? Tough! If they wanted the parking space, they should have tried a little harder!

CERTIFICATE OF OWNERSHIP
YOUR OWN PARKING SPOT RIGHT NEXT TO YOUR OFFICE

No more lateness, no more of that unpleasant cardiovascular exercise walking from your car to the building entrance—and *everyone* will know who you are! Some of your coworkers are a little envious? Tough! If they wanted the parking space, they should have tried a little harder!

CERTIFICATE OF OWNERSHIP
RELOCATION TO THE CITY OF YOUR CHOICE

New York, Paris, Hong Kong, the Cayman Islands—now's your chance to live out your dreams! Be ready to leave family and friends behind (you'll certainly see them again, *often,* over the years). For now, get ready to experience something many people only imagine. Seek out brave, new worlds, go where no one has gone before! The Force be with you. ...

CERTIFICATE OF OWNERSHIP
YOUR OWN EXECUTIVE BATHROOM WITH JACUZZI

Okay, so most execs seldom have time to use these suckers—you know *you* will. (And if not, you can at least brag that you have one. That should increase your popularity tremendously!)

CERTIFICATE OF OWNERSHIP
A GOURMET LUNCH, COOKED TO YOUR ORDER AND BROUGHT TO YOU EVERY DAY

Enough cafeteria fare! Some of us just *appreciate* fine food. No doubt about it, this goody will add significantly to your quality of life at work. (You need only take the appropriate steps to ward off the weight gain that could possibly accompany it.)

CERTIFICATE OF OWNERSHIP
YOUR OWN CORNER OFFICE WITH WINDOWS, FOUR WALLS, AND A LOCKED DOOR

Ah, privacy! It's great to be out of the general work area, with its chatter and gossip. Even if it's *you* they sometimes talk about now that you're "removed," who cares? You can rely on the head honchos of your organization to know any petty backbiting is untrue.

CERTIFICATE OF OWNERSHIP
TELECOMMUTING

Working from home is pure bliss. Get up and stretch when you wish; roam to your well-stocked refrigerator at will; play any music you like from your own personal CD collection. There is certainly no danger of *distractions*— you can easily turn off *Oprah* when the work at hand needs your attention!

CERTIFICATE OF OWNERSHIP
A KEY TO THE COMPANY-OWNED APARTMENT

Great for impressing clients, sleeping after 16-hour work days, and plain old midday napping. The fact is, there's *nothing* like executive perks. (And un-doubtedly your marriage is strong enough so that your spouse won't won-der what other opportunities that apartment affords you. ...)

CERTIFICATE OF OWNERSHIP
A GENEROUS CLOTHING ALLOWANCE

Nothing's better than knowing you look like a million bucks—unless it's knowing you did it with someone else's money! So what if your bosses and coworkers scrutinize your appearance more critically than they used to—*you* know you have great taste. Bring on the Fashion Police. ...

CERTIFICATE OF OWNERSHIP
A COMPANY CAR, WITH DRIVER, TO TAKE YOU TO AND FROM WORK

Leave road rage to someone else! Instead, spend that valuable energy—and commute time—working on company business. (This *is* what your employ-ers expected when they gave you the car, of course.)

CERTIFICATE OF OWNERSHIP
FLEX-TIME

Praise heaven! No more fuming in rush-hour gridlock every day. So you have to get up at 4 a.m., or leave work at 8 p.m. Think of the commute hours saved in a year.

CERTIFICATE OF OWNERSHIP
CUSTOMERS AND COLLEAGUES SO PLEASANT THEY COULD LIVE N MR. ROGERS' NEIGHBORHOOD

Could there possibly be a downside to this? Heaven knows, we can't think of one. ...

CERTIFICATE OF OWNERSHIP
A BOSS SO PLEASANT S/HE TAUGHT MR. ROGERS HOW TO BE NICE

Ditto.

CERTIFICATE OF OWNERSHIP
THE FASTEST, MOST USER-FRIENDLY COMPUTER IN YOUR WHOLE COMPANY

Yee-hah! Finally you can get some work done! This will improve your quality of life tremendously. So you can *certainly* afford to be gracious when coworkers beg to log on any time you step away from your desk.

CERTIFICATE OF OWNERSHIP
TWO MONTHS PAID VACATION PER YEAR

No more of those paltry, two-week deals that usually end up as nerve-racking obligatory visits with relatives. This is *real* R&R—a break from the rat race. Take advantage! Do *not* spend it worrying about petty things like 1) returning to a Mount Everest of untouched paperwork on your desk, or, worse still, 2) that everyone is getting along just fine without you.

CERTIFICATE OF OWNERSHIP
A 200% RAISE IN SALARY

This will, of course, bring you more of the material comforts you want and deserve—even if it also creates the need to find more write-offs that will give you the lowest possible tax burden (*and* the lowest possible chance of being audited). But what's a little accounting hassle? Remember that your family will admire and love you for your prowess as a breadwinner, even as their demands increase for clothes, cars, and other things they know you will provide with your *next* big raise.

CERTIFICATE OF OWNERSHIP
A COMPANY DAYCARE CENTER, WITH A
VERITABLE "MARY POPPINS" STAFF

You get to see your kids on breaks; you'll be informed immediately about illnesses, injuries, and other things. What a load off your mind! Your children may learn to seek love and affection from their daycare staff instead of from *you*. But hey, isn't this exactly what the Royal Family goes through?

CERTIFICATE OF OWNERSHIP
SKILLS TRAINING ON DEMAND

The skills in your current position constantly need updating. In addition, you never know when you'll be thinking about "moving on." The fact is, ongoing training seems the best route to high employability. On the other hand, sitting through boring seminars and workshops has so far been about as enjoyable as having your fingernails pulled out. Are you sure it's worth it?

CERTIFICATE OF OWNERSHIP
BIG-TIME HEALTH BENEFITS

Never fill out another form! Just bring your health card with you on any visit to your MD, dentist, chiropractor or massage therapist, and pay only 20% of cost. (Also, never quit your job—after all, you'd have to be insane to give up all this!

CERTIFICATE OF OWNERSHIP
REGULAR, PRIVATE MEETINGS WITH YOUR CEO, WHO MUST ACT ON ALL YOUR MANDATES

Isn't it about time someone who really understands the nuts and bolts got some say? Your coworkers will love you—*and* the chance to finally have the ear of "one of their own." They'll seek you out constantly. And undoubtedly they'll stand by you if some of their ideas that you passed on don't work out too well!

CERTIFICATE OF OWNERSHIP
APPOINTMENT AS PRESIDENT OF YOUR COMPANY'S BOARD OF DIRECTORS

Respect, power, challenge—it just doesn't get any better. All those late-night and weekend meetings will be no problem—just watch out for those backroom politics! (Some of those other, empire-building board members can be *vicious*.)

GAME 2—THE FEAR DRAG

THE POINT OF THIS GAME

People who successfully handle change can **deal effectively with fear**. Fear is often the only thing (or at least the main thing) that prevents us from successfully embarking on a new direction. In fact, researchers suggest that in order for a person to make a change, the fear of *not* changing must be greater than the fear of changing! This game illustrates the results of letting fear lead us and offers an alternative way of dealing with fear.

TIME NEEDED

15–25 minutes, depending on debriefing

MATERIALS NEEDED

- Two to six bandannas or paper bags
- 15 to 30 candies or other treats. (*Note:* we find Tootsie Roll Pops™ are particularly well-received.) The number of candies will depend on room size, available time, and number of participants.
- Baggies into which team members can put the treats as they find them
- A watch or timer
- A whistle or other noisemaker

A SUGGESTED FUNNY INTRODUCTION

[*Note:* This introduction lets you get laughs by having fun—creating curiosity and anticipation—rather than by being funny.

Start by selecting 4 to 12 learners and pairing them up. Then say:]

"Meet your Navigation Partner. One of you is Person A, and the other is Person B. Let's decide who's who right now. Person A is the one with the shortest or else most brightly-polished nails. Check it out now. [Let them do so. Then, handing the bandanna or paper bag to Person A:] This is a blindfold. You will receive further instructions about it shortly. For now, please leave the room with your partner and wait outside. We will call you when we are ready."

HOW TO PLAY THIS GAME

1. As soon as the teams have left, have the rest of your learners swing into action: Half of them place the candies around the room in fairly hard-to-reach spots, while the other half quickly set up chairs and other objects as obstacles. *Note: Be careful to keep the room setup physically safe!* The candies and obstacles should represent a challenge, not an impossibility or a danger. Let your learners use their imaginations, but keep a sharp eye on their choices. As soon as the room is ready, go to the door and tell Persons A to blindfold Persons B and lead them in.

2. Ask Persons A to grab hold of the arm or shirtsleeve of their blindfolded partners.

3. Tell the teams that there are fabulous prizes scattered throughout the room, and it is their job to collect as many as they can within 3 minutes. The hitch: Each pair must remain physically connected at all times. Persons B, who are blindfolded, will lead. Persons B are the only ones who can actually pick up the treats, which they will then hand over to their partners. Persons A cannot give any directions to their partners. They can only confirm with yes or no answers any questions their partners direct to them. ("Should I move to the left?" or "Will I hit something if I go too many steps?") The other learners can shout out helpful suggestions about where to look. (Tell them this increases the chance that the grateful team members will share their booty.) Give the teams 3 minutes to gather their candies.

4. Blow the whistle to begin the game.

5. After 3 minutes, blow the whistle again. Ask each pair to count the number of candies they collected.

6. Tell the teams it is time for Round 2. This time, Persons A give as detailed directions as they like to their partners. Blow the whistle, let them go for 3 minutes, then call time. Persons B can now remove their blindfolds, and the teams return to their seats. Again, count the number of candies collected. See who got the most fabulous prizes and give them a cheer. Let the teams hand out candies to anyone who helped them.

DEBRIEFING QUESTIONS

- **KEY POINT:** This game symbolized how fear affects our efforts to go after what we want. Person A was the part of us with the information; Person B was the physical symbol of fear, bound intrinsically to the partner; the treats represented goals we want to achieve in life. Almost any new endeavor involves some fear—fear of failure, fear of change, fear of the unknown. Fear always slows us down, makes us move more cautiously, so it can rightly be called a "drag" on our movements. But sometimes *we* drag fear around, and sometimes we let it drag *us* around. In the first round, fear was in control. In the second, we were still attached to our fear but this time our intellect was in control.

- To Persons A: What was it like for you in the first round when you could only respond to your partners' questions? How effective were you in getting toward your goal of collecting candy? In which round did you collect more candy?

- To Persons A: What were your thoughts and feelings during the game? Anyone feel frustrated by having to drag around your partner? Did you think, "Come on, it's easy"? Have you ever looked back on a past fear and thought, "Why was I afraid? It was easy"? Was there anything that you said to your partner in this game that could be useful if you said it to yourself in real life?

116

- To Persons B: What were your thoughts and feelings during the game? How did it feel to wear the blindfold? What thoughts and feelings did you experience as you moved around? [Learners will probably observe that they felt helpless, out of control, frustrated.]
- What did you wish your partner could have said to help you navigate your way? How would this have helped?
- To the class as a whole: How did the blindfold affect the pairs? What did you notice about the way the pairs interacted with each other the first time? The second time?
- When you are in a new situation, do you ever feel as if you are blindfolded?
- How does fear in real life get in the way of our ability to achieve our goals?
- Why do we drag around fear in real life? What if anything does fear do *for* us? [Most learners will probably answer that fear protects us from making dangerous decisions. Ask if it is fear that protects us or simply intelligence and common sense.]
- Would you be doing anything differently in your life or in your job if you weren't afraid? Do you think your fear is valid or not? **KEY POINT:** Are you dragging your fear around, or is it dragging *you*?

TIPS ON MAKING THIS GAME WORK WELL

With smaller groups, all your learners can play. Make sure there are enough candies scattered around so that each pair can collect about five pieces each round.

OTHER TOPICS THIS GAME TEACHES

- Assertiveness
- Reducing Workplace Negativity
- Emotional Intelligence

GAME 3—WEDDING GUESTS

THE POINT OF THIS GAME

People (and organizations) that deal well with change **are prepared for the inevitable emotional stages** of the process. In her seminal research on grief and death, Dr. Elizabeth Kubler-Ross chronicled six recognizable stages. They are: denial, anger, bargaining, depression, acceptance, and hope.* These stages seem most likely to manifest when 1) change is *externally imposed* and 2) *something of value is being lost or given up* as a result of the change. This game creates awareness of these stages, making learners better prepared to deal with them as their organizations undergo change. (*Note:* It's also a great game for sharing the spotlight with your learners!)

TIME NEEDED

20 minutes

MATERIALS NEEDED

- The six stages displayed on a flip chart, whiteboard, or overhead, but not in their correct chronological order.
- Party invitation with role description for each learner. See handouts. (*Note:* There are six possible roles. You can have multiple guests playing the same role in large groups, but make sure each role is represented at least once.)

*For more information, see E. Kubler-Ross, *On Death and Dying,* New York: Macmillan, 1969.

118

- A blank index card for each learner
- A pen or pencil for each learner

A SUGGESTED FUNNY INTRODUCTION

"Has anyone ever been to a wedding reception where you'd swear some of the guests were crashers? [Show of hands.] Would two or three people like to tell us about it? [Allow two or three minutes for learners to share tales of "Horrible Wedding Guests I Have Known." This will get big laughs, and build rapport within the group.] Well, we are now going to create our own *Wedding Reception from Hell.* This event is truly outstanding in the fact that almost *all* of the guests are a *complete* embarrassment to the bride and groom. Most are totally against this marriage for one reason or another. Some of them are depressed, others refuse to believe it's happening at all, still others are just in an all-out rotten mood. Wouldn't you love to mingle with these folks for a little while? Well here's your chance! Welcome to ... *the Wedding Reception from Hell.*"

HOW TO PLAY THIS GAME

1. Hand out the party invitations to the learners so that each role is represented at least once. Give learners a moment to read their role descriptions.

2. Optional, but *highly* recommended: Distribute one index card to each learner, and ask learners to write down their names and the weirdest or tackiest wedding gift someone might give a bride and groom. (Tell them they get extra points if their gift was actually given to a real-life couple!) At any point they choose during the reception, they will give the gifts to the trainer, who will be acting as the bride or groom.

3. Tell the group that the wedding ceremony has just ended and the reception has begun. Everyone is milling around, imbibing champagne and finger foods, and chatting. As they talk together, learners must express the emotions written on their invitations. (Tell them to exaggerate a bit—bonus

points for good impressions!) They must remain in conversation until both parties identify each other's emotions. Once they both think they've figured out each other's emotions, they say something like "Gee, you must be angry/in denial/depressed," and move on to someone else.

4. Stop the reception after 7 to 10 minutes. Thank the guests for attending, and have them sit down.

5. Ask for one volunteer representing each of the stages to stand at the front of the room. With the group's help and directions, ask the volunteers to place themselves in what they believe is the correct chronological order.*

6. When the learners accomplish this, ask each volunteer to describe his or her stage (they can use their invitations if necessary). Thank the volunteers and ask them to sit down.

7. After the debriefing, "open" the wedding gifts by reading the index cards to the group at large.

DEBRIEFING QUESTIONS

- What interesting things happened during this game?
- What were some of the things people said or did during the reception that helped you to identify them?
- How do people express these stages in real life? What behavioral clues do they give?
- Why might people go through these stages in this order? For instance, why is denial first? Why would depression follow bargaining? [Possible answers: Depression follows bargaining because the person recognizes the lack of control in the situation. This depresses them as they grapple with the new reality.]
- What stage do you believe your organization is in? Where are you?

*The correct order is: denial, anger, bargaining, depression, acceptance, hope. This can be remembered through the cool acronym HAD BAD which is composed of the first letter of each word, starting from hope and going backward.

- What advice might you give to someone who is at the anger or depression stage?
- What do people need from each other in order to move through to the last stage, hope?
- What insights did you get from this game?

TIPS ON MAKING THIS GAME WORK WELL

The trainer helps the learners feel more comfortable about play-acting by taking on the role of the bride or groom. The symbolic gift-giving grounds the learners into the experience by providing a tangible action. The trainer can also use this interchange to introduce and pair up more hesitant learners. And, of course, "opening" the gifts at the end of the game is a guaranteed laugh-getter!

OTHER TOPICS THIS GAME TEACHES

- Emotional Intelligence
- Reducing Workplace Negativity
- Dealing with Stress

You are cordially invited to the wedding of Mary Me and Deke Out-Now.

You are the bride or groom's best friend and you strongly dislike your friend's new spouse. Your role: DENIAL. During this stage we typically act as if nothing is wrong, that the situation or change won't affect us. Essentially, we are *avoiding* dealing with the changing situation. Typical language: "Well so what if s/he's married now? We'll still go out bar-hopping every weekend, just like we always have." "My friend is just getting married to get better health insurance. S/he's not really in love." "I can eat another four pieces of cake—the calories that you eat at weddings don't count." "Just because I'm sobbing doesn't mean I'm upset. I'm fine. Really. I'm *happy* for them, dammit."

You are cordially invited to the wedding of Mary Me and Deke Out-Now.

You are the jilted lover of the bride or groom. Your role: ANGER. During this stage, we finally acknowledge that the situation has changed, but we feel helpless and frustrated about it. We may believe that we are losing something that is important to us, and resent that we are powerless to stop it. Typical language: "I cannot *believe* these two bozos are getting married." "I've been to better receptions at funerals." "Nothing good will come of this." "These two have nothing in common. I give the marriage one month."

You are cordially invited to the wedding of Mary Me and Deke Out-Now.

You are the wary godmother or godfather of the bride. You know she could have done better than this loser. Your role: BARGAINING. During this stage, we feel some guilt and confusion. We want to regain some sense of control, so we bargain or make "deals" to prevent the situation from getting out of hand. These deals can be with God or with ourselves, as well as with others. Typical language: "Well, I'll let her stick this marriage out till after the honeymoon, and *then* we'll see." "I'll just bide my time until she comes to her senses, and meanwhile I'll see if her cousin Marvin still has a crush on her." "If God gets me out of these uncomfortable shoes, I won't ask for one more thing, ever."

You are cordially invited to the wedding of Mary Me and Deke Out-Now.

You are a single cousin of the groom and you wish you were getting married. Your role: DEPRESSION. During this stage, we've come to see that the changing situation is not likely to reverse itself, and we feel sad. We may or may not be aware that this is what we're feeling, and our depression can manifest itself though behavior like sleeping too much or too little, withdrawal, overeating (hint for the roleplay: or over*drinking*). Typical language: "No, I'm too tired to do the hokey pokey. I'll sit here and write an ode to death." "Looks like I broke a heel of my expensive new shoe. Oh, well, who cares?" "Is there someplace I can go and lie down for awhile?" "It's hopeless, I'll never get married. Where's my Prozac?"

You are cordially invited to the wedding of Mary Me and Deke Out-Now.

You are a longtime friend of the bride or groom. Your role: ACCEPTANCE. At this stage we are coming to grips with the changing situation. We focus our efforts on regaining our sense of power, and look for new ways to take care of our needs. Typical language: "Well, okay, apparently I am the only single person here. Hmm—maybe someone in the band is available?" "Well, I might as well get over him or her now that s/he is married." "Maybe there's someone here who can get me a better job. Where are my business cards?"

You are cordially invited to the wedding of Mary Me and Deke Out-Now.

You are the kid brother or sister of the groom. Your role: HOPE. At this stage, we have become reconciled to the new situation and feel a sense of optimism. We start looking at how this situation might create great new opportunities for the future. We may be seen by others as an informal leader, able to help them to cope better. Typical language: "I'm so excited about getting a new sister! We can be best friends." "Just think, I get to have his room!" "Wow, if someone is willing to marry a dork like my *brother*, then *I* should have no problem."

GAME 4—MAY THE FORCES BE WITH YOU

THE POINT OF THIS GAME

People (and organizations) who succeed in making lasting changes know how to **accurately assess the pros and cons**. They analyze a complex and sometimes bewildering system of opposing forces, some in favor of change and some against. It's these forces that actually hold us back from or help propel us toward a solution. In other words, we decide to move ahead only when the forces *for* change outweigh the forces *against*. But we can only make that decision when we clearly understand these forces and their impact on the situation.

This game introduces learners to Kurt Lewin's Force Field Analysis* and demonstrates how to apply this theory to real life situations—that is, how to clearly identify the forces or causes behind a situation. The game can also serve as an introduction to an action planning session.

TIME NEEDED

40 minutes

MATERIALS NEEDED

- Masking tape
- Index card-sized Post-It notes
- Two flip charts or several sheets of paper

*For more information on the Force Field Analysis theory, see Kurt Lewin, *Field Theory in Social Science*, New York, *Harper*, 1951.

- 3 x 5-inch cards
- Markers and pens

PREPARATION

You will need considerable wall space and tape for this game. Tear off a long strip of masking tape (at least 8 feet) and tape it horizontally across the wall. Tear off a shorter piece of tape (about 6 inches) and place it vertically at the center of the line. Using the Post-It notes, label one side of the wall Driving Forces and the other side Restraining Forces. Place smaller strips of masking tape on this line at 6-inch or 12-inch increments to indicate degrees. You will need at least 10 degrees on each side, so your choice of how much space to give each increment depends on how long your horizontal line is. Place a Post-It note on the center spot where the two taped lines intersect.

SUGGESTED FUNNY INTRODUCTION

"Abraham Lincoln once said, 'If I had eight hours to chop down a tree, I'd spend six hours sharpening my ax.' Many people would do it differently. They'd spend twenty minutes on the ax—and twelve hours hacking at the tree!

"The good news is, most of us will never have to chop down a tree. But we do have *other* challenges, and too often we don't plan our solutions carefully enough. We get a headache. We take an aspirin. The headache doesn't go away. We take another aspirin. It still doesn't go away. We ... [Let learners fill in: "Take another aspirin."] Right. Still doesn't go away. Finally we ... [Learners fill in the rest. Most answers will express impotent frustration, like, "Give up" or "Go to bed." Some learners will almost certainly try venting humor: "Take a drink!" "Take a swing at the cat!" As always, laugh at their jokes—as long as they are not inappropriate.]

"You get the idea. The point is that often we act on the *first solution that occurs to us.* And if the problem doesn't *immediately* disappear, we either give up, or do exactly what we tried before, only harder. Just like taking an aspirin for a headache caused by stress, you might actually be focused on a *symptom* of the problem, and not the real *cause.*

"How many would agree that before we tackle our problems, we'd better be sure about our solutions? [Show of hands.] Okay! Let's play a game that shows us how."

HOW TO PLAY THIS GAME

1. Choose a situation common to all the learners. This situation should represent a problem, something that all can agree needs to be changed. Word it as specifically as possible: "Increase employee retention by 20 percent" or "Increase participation and efficiency at staff meetings" or "Lose 10 pounds." Write this problem on the center Post-It note. (*Note:* You can also phrase the situation as a question: "How do we get our best employees to stay with us longer?")

2. Ask for three volunteers who will be the judges. Divide the rest of the learners into two teams:

   Team A is the Restraining Force. Their mission is to identify all the forces that keep the problem from being addressed and improved upon. These can range from emotional, personal issues to systemic, organizational forces.

   Team B is the Driving Force. This group's mission is to identify all the forces that encourage or support change.

3. Give the teams 20 minutes to brainstorm and list their forces on the flip charts or sheets of paper. After 20 minutes, ask the teams to stop brainstorming. Direct them to divvy up the forces so that each learner holds one. (You may have individuals holding two more cards, or groups in which not everyone has a card.)

4. Give the teams one minute to come up with their own, unique team names.

5. Advise the learners that this is not a competitive game! In other words, a team doesn't "win" if the Post-It ends up on their side of the dividing line. Teams *do* get points, however, for the team cheer and for the presentation of their force.

6. The three volunteer judges have two important decisions to make. The first is to decide the strength of the force on a scale of 1 to 10. Forces that have a tremendous impact on the effort to change are rated 10 and those that seem to have little effect are rated 1. (*Note:* The numbers assigned are *not* comparative to each other. In other words, two forces could be considered a 7 in strength, none might be considered a 10 or a 1, and so on.) The judges have 30 seconds to reach a consensus decision on the strength of the force. The judges' decisions are final and the learners should be discouraged from disputing the amount awarded.

7. The second thing the judges decide on is how creatively and dramatically a team member presented the force. As in the Olympics, the judges can award 1 to 5 points. You can give the judges prepared placards for this, or each judge can vote by holding up the appropriate number of fingers. You will need to keep track of the cumulative total of points for each team.

8. Ask each team to introduce themselves and explain their team name.

9. Turn to the Driving Force and ask the team member holding the most powerful card to introduce himself or herself as the force listed, and describe that power in three colorful sentences or less. For example: "I am Government Regulations—*tremble in fear!* If you do not satisfy my demand for change, you could lose your funding *and* the whole program."

10. Ask the judges to make a consensus decision on the strength of this driving force and have the team member

move the center Post-It that number of degrees along the taped line.

11. Ask the judges to vote on the dramatic or humorous presentation of this force. Count the cumulative total for the presentation piece. The team cheers as the member struts back to join them.

12. Now it's Restraining Force's turn to retaliate. They send up their most powerful force and follow the same process, except that they will be moving the Post-It toward their own side of the room. Note that their force may be more or less powerful than the previous Driving Force. For example, if their force is 8, while the Driving Force was 10, the Post-It would remain on the Driving Force side of the room, at least for the time being.

13. Continue until all the forces have been presented. Note the final position of the Post-It (i.e., on which side of the room it finally rests).

14. Count up the points the teams accumulated for their presentations and applaud the winning team.

DEBRIEFING QUESTIONS

- What thoughts did you have as you watched the Post-It being moved?

- Did the Post-It ultimately end up where you predicted prior to the game? How did you feel about where it did end up? Were you glad? Disappointed?

- How did this game affect or change your perceptions about this situation? In your opinion, which forces seem to have the most influence on this situation?

- Which restraining forces do you think you need to address in order to move forward?

- Which driving forces do you need to strengthen?

- What would you see as the next step you or your organization should take after identifying *your* driving and restraining forces?

TIPS ON MAKING THIS GAME WORK WELL

The game will get bogged down if the teams dispute the number of degrees each force is awarded. Remind the teams that they don't win if the Post-It ends up on their side. This game will only be useful if teams give an honest assessment about the strength of the forces. Encourage the teams to discuss any disagreements during the debriefing. In fact, we suggest that for the debriefing you ask the learners to sit in a circle or horseshoe to symbolize that they are not in opposition to each other in resolving the situation.

Following this game, you may want to strategize with the learners on which restraining forces to weaken and which driving forces to strengthen. This game does not serve as a problem-solving activity in itself; it is a tool to analyze and assess the factors affecting a situation. This game acts as a fun introduction to a strategizing session.

Note: Thanks to Cindy McCann, Custom Performance Solutions, Inc., for inspiring this game.

OTHER TOPICS THIS GAME TEACHES

- Conflict and Negotiation
- Emotional Intelligence
- Management Skills
- Reducing Workplace Negativity

GAME 5—SQUISHY TOY COMPANY

THE POINT OF THIS GAME

People who are strong change-managers are **resilient in weathering sudden shifts in direction.** This resiliency is marked by the all-too-rare ability to adapt quickly and respond effectively and comfortably to new information.

This game simulates many workplaces today, where organizational groups must often respond to repeated directional shifts, many times without understanding all the reasons behind the change. It illustrates how shifts in direction affect performance, group, and interpersonal dynamics.

TIME NEEDED

Approximately 50 minutes

MATERIALS NEEDED

- A diverse assortment of playful "supplies": rubber bands, construction paper, pennies, buttons, playing cards, pipe cleaners, dice, scissors, tape
- A Team Description card for each learner (see handouts)
- Three Information cards (see handouts)
- Two egg timers

PREPARATION

Place all the "supplies" on a large table where most of your learners—the Development Team—will sit. Distribute the Team

Description cards, and ask the learners to find and sit with other members of their team. (*Note:* The Development Team gets the table with the supplies. The other two teams should sit as far away from each other as the room will allow. You can even place these two small groups in break-out rooms. Place the egg timers near these two groups.)

A SUGGESTED FUNNY INTRODUCTION

[*Note:* Do *not* summarize the learning objectives! Instead, simply begin the game by introducing yourself as "your respected founder and CEO of the Squishy Toy Company," and welcoming them to this special planning session. Then say:]

"As you all know, our business faces tough times. Tough, very tough. Our main competitor, Oozing Toy Company, is gaining on us with it new game, Martian Manhunt. Your mission today is to develop our next breakthrough game, one that will knock out Oozing like an Uzi. Ha, ha. [Wait for laughter from your underlings. If they don't laugh, glare at them. If they do, smile warmly.]

"We need to introduce this new game to the market as soon as possible. I'm sure I don't have to remind you how important it is for us to keep our dominant industry position. If we don't have a major success—*soon*—we may have to lay off employees. We might even have to get rid of our cappuccino machine.

"Our research department has determined the most popular materials that need to be in our next game. They are all here on this table. [Indicate the Development Team's table.]

"First I want to introduce the groups in the room. We have here our genius Squishy Development Team, who will use the next 20 minutes to design our new game, using at least some (and hopefully all) of the materials on their table. We also have our hardworking Squishy Supervisors, who will provide direction and assistance to our Development Team. Finally, we are honored to have with us our visionary Squishy Presidents, who will provide us with some strategic direction for this game.

"As you all know, it's the job of our Squishy Development Team to work together to come up with a winning game, *complete with name*. As usual, they also get a big bonus for coming up with a *commercial jingle* that will sell this game. And as usual, they will present all these ideas to the Supervisors and Presidents for their approval.

"We only have 20 minutes to develop this game and its advertising. But I know you are creative people, and will have no problem coming up with our next best-seller in that time.

"So, Squishy Development, please get started on your work right now. Squishy Supervisors, please observe their progress and offer any suggestions you like. Meanwhile, I will meet with the Squishy Presidents. ..."

HOW TO PLAY THIS GAME

ROUND 1:

1. Give all the materials to the Development Team and tell them to start creating their toy or game.

2. Take the Presidents group to a far corner of the room and read them the Round One Information Card aloud. After you finish, they have 2 minutes to make a decision about the gender target. They will then communicate their decision to the Supervisory Team. Start the egg timer and walk away, leaving the Information Card with them.

3. When the egg timer goes off, have the Presidents immediately call the Supervisors to their table and share their decision with them.

4. The Supervisors now have two tasks: to make their own decision on what age range the game should target and to update the Development Team. They will have 2 minutes for this. Set the egg timer and walk away.

ROUND 2:

5. Go back to the Presidents and give them the Round 2 Information Card. Set the egg timer for 2 minutes. When 2

133

minutes are up, they must communicate their new decision to the Supervisors.

6. The Supervisors now have 2 minutes to make a decision, which they must then communicate to the Development Team.

ROUND 3:

7. Go back to the Presidents and give them the Round 3 Information Card. Set the egg timer for 2 minutes. When 2 minutes are up they must communicate their new decision to the Supervisors.

8. Call time after 20 minutes. Have the Development Team describe or play the game for the Presidents and Supervisors and perform the jingle, if they have one. Lead the applause and thank everyone.

DEBRIEFING QUESTIONS

- **KEY POINT:** The process of change often does feel "squishy" or uncertain. New strategies are untested, their outcomes unclear. We are in a position of acting without knowing. Human beings usually feel uncomfortable in this process.
- What were you thinking or feeling at the beginning of the activity? Near the end? Why did your thoughts and feelings change?
- What happened in your group as this activity progressed? How did the group dynamics change?
- What happened to the game you were developing? Did you end up with a successful game? Why or why not?
- What information could have helped the Development Team? The Supervisors? The Presidents?
- How did this activity relate to your real-world experiences in dealing with change? How did this game model how your organization communicates changes in direction?

134

- How do tight deadlines affect people's emotional resiliency, social skills, and ability to think well? Is it different for different people?

- What did you observe about yourself and how you dealt with the continual changes and challenges of this activity? What was similar to or different from how you approach change in real life?

- **KEY POINT:** What could you *personally* do differently in your workplace, right now, to help yourself or others respond to sudden changes in direction?

TIPS ON MAKING THIS GAME WORK WELL

To keep the game moving quickly, give the Presidents new Information Cards as soon as they end their meetings with the Supervisors. Your role is to read the card to them, start the timer, and walk away.

You can play this game another way that is equally interesting: Don't give the Presidents and Supervisors any time limits! Simply remind them at the outset that if they take too long in up-front meetings, the Development Team will ultimately have that much less time to adapt. (Note that if you play the game this way, your debriefing should then include a discussion of what is gained and lost by spending more time on up-front decision making.)

Both homogeneous and heterogeneous groups can play this game with illuminating effects. For example, a homogeneous group of real-life presidents or directors would gain much insight into the effects of sudden change on their staff. This game can be particularly powerful with *heterogeneous* groups (preferably at a retreat). Be sure to randomly select which attendees will play Presidents, Supervisors and Development Team members—for example through lottery—and make sure to set it up well with an introduction that emphasizes the value of "walking in another's shoes."

OTHER TOPICS THIS GAME TEACHES

- Creative Problem Solving
- Management Skills
- Reducing Workplace Negativity
- Dealing with Stress

SQUISHY ROLE DESCRIPTIONS

(Three-quarters of your learners should receive these.)

Squishy Development Team Member:

You're a dedicated and creative member of the Development Team at Squishy Toy Company. You and your team work well together, and have designed some of Squishy's best-selling toys in the past. As always, you feel confident in your abilities to handle today's project.

(Two to four learners should receive these.)

Squishy Supervisor:

You're a dedicated supervisor at Squishy Toys. You like and trust the Development Team members you supervise. It's your job to communicate the decisions made by the Presidents to the Development Team.

(Two to four learners should receive these.)

Squishy President

You're a dedicated president at Squishy Toy Company. Your job is to respond to the constant changes in the marketplace, to keep Squishy flexible and competitive. This means that you and your fellow presidents have to make tough decisions quickly, often in response to late-breaking information.

SQUISHY INFORMATION CARDS (GIVEN TO THE PRESIDENTS GROUP)

Round One Information Card:

The marketing department has just determined that in order for this game to be a best-seller, it must be specifically targeted to either boys or girls. You have two minutes to decide which gender should be targeted. When two minutes are up, call a meeting with the Supervisors and inform them of your decision. Tell the supervisors that it is now their job to 1) make a decision on the age range the game should appeal to and 2) inform the Development Team of these decisions. They will have a total of two minutes to make their decisions and talk to the Development Team.

Round Two Information Card:

After a thorough analysis, Accounting has determined that you will need to cut business costs by 50 percent. You have two minutes to determine how to cut costs: personnel or toy materials. (You do not need to decide which personnel or materials will have to go.) Tell the Supervisors your decision, and that it's their job to decide how to implement your decision.

Round Three Information Card:

You hear shocking news that Oozing Toy Company is going to market a game using the very same materials as your new game! Marketing believes that your game must have a really snappy name to distinguish it as the better game. You have two minutes to come up with a name for the new game. Inform the Supervisors of your decision, and that it will be their job to come up with a way that the Development Team can adapt the game to fit the new name.

6

Five Games to Develop Relaxed, Engaging Speakers

GAME 1—PHRASE BALL

THE POINT OF THIS GAME

Truly personable speakers are **spontaneous**. They seem to relish those extemporaneous moments that happen in every presentation—in fact, they seek them out! They invite questions; they respond avidly to audience comments. They pop out with unplanned ad libs. (Yes, some ad libs *are* unplanned!) All this serves to set them apart from the standard fare of speakers: They really capture and hold an audiences' attention, and breathe life into a room. As a result, their message is usually *received and remembered better.*

This game, with its constant ball-tossing, will help to distract your learners from any fears they might have about spontaneity, thus letting them more easily reclaim their natural gift with it.

TIME NEEDED

15–20 minutes

MATERIALS NEEDED

A Nerf™ (or other soft) ball

A SUGGESTED FUNNY INTRODUCTION

"What's the difference between a new keynote speaker and a deer caught in the headlights? The deer *sometimes* reacts to the sound of an air horn."

HOW TO PLAY THIS GAME

1. Have your learners stand in a circle. Tell them that they will now discover how talented they are at speaking extemporaneously.

2. The members of the circle will toss the ball to one another, at the same time speaking a simple, descriptive phrase: "the placid lake,""the little girl,""the beautiful city skyline,""the terrifying grizzly," "the soft Nerf™ ball," etc. *Tell them that since there are no rules, there are also no wrong phrases!* Have the group take turns tossing and speaking until everyone has gotten confident with the ability to quickly come up with a phrase (this usually takes less than 5 minutes). When you feel this has happened, wait for the next time the ball gets tossed to you, and hold onto it.

3. Congratulate them all on their verbal virtuosity, and tell them they have moved ahead to the advanced level with astonishing speed. Tell them they will now play the game again, this time with only one rule: *Their phrases must relate to the one that came before.* That is, one person will utter a phrase and toss the ball, and the person catching it will *add onto* that phrase.

4. Try a couple of passes. Toss the ball and say: "the idle cannibal ..." The person catching it must now say something like, "picking his teeth." (Applaud him or her to encourage the rest.) This person will then throw the ball to someone else, saying, perhaps, "the soft, summer clouds ..." Whoever catches the ball says, "floating across the sky." That person turns and tosses it to someone else, saying, "the angry two-year-old ..." That person catches it and says, "yelling her head off." And so on.

5. Do this until, once again, everyone seems comfortable with the ability to speak extemporaneously, at least most of the time. Express your admiration and ask your learners to sit down.

DEBRIEFING QUESTIONS

- What were your thoughts or feelings when the ball got tossed to you? Did these change as the game progressed?
- How comfortable were you in coming up with something to say in the moment? Did you censor or evaluate your contributions?
- Which round was easier for you, round one or two? As a speaker, how could your presentations improve if you focused on *responding* to your groups instead of impressing them?
- How does all this apply to making your presentations? Does being spontaneous mean you shouldn't carefully prepare? [Answer: No!]
- **KEY POINT:** Once you've prepared—written, rewritten, and rehearsed your presentation—what do you have to do next? [Answer: Get ready to play with the unexpected ... because it *will* happen!]

TIPS ON MAKING THIS GAME WORK WELL

If any of your learners consistently have trouble with this game, it is usually because they are pressuring themselves to be clever—to come up with poetic, funny, or unusual phrases. Keep reminding these people that the point of this game is *spontaneity* (i.e., an open-minded curiosity about what will happen next), not *originality*. Tell them they don't have to worry about their originality. It will show up by itself; in fact, they can't repress it. For the moment, their challenge is to dare to be banal—to just go with the first idea that occurs to them. Then swallow your pride and model this for them every time the ball comes your way!

OTHER TOPICS THIS GAME TEACHES

- How to Be a Naturally Funny Trainer
- Facilitation Skills

GAME 2—GIBBERISH EXPERTS

THE POINT OF THIS GAME

Truly personable speakers know how to **physically relax** for their presentations.

Why? Because they know how much this physical state will enhance the *nonverbal* parts of their communication—the parts you can't fake, and that audiences receive at the powerful, subliminal level. With relaxation, good oratory skills seem to emerge of their own accord: These speakers' bodies become more fluid, their voices more open-throated, their eye contact more frequent and genuine. All of this invites their audiences to connect with them—and consequently to feel *more positively inclined toward their message.*

This game allows your learners to experience genuine relaxation in the speaking situation. It also visually demonstrates the value of doing so.

TIME NEEDED

50 minutes to an hour, depending on the number of learners to tape

MATERIALS NEEDED

- A video camera
- A playback monitor
- Enough tape to record each learner for a total of 2 minutes
- Two 3 x 5-inch cards for each learner

A SUGGESTED FUNNY INTRODUCTION

[*Note:* We find it best to do the following without explanation. The lack of context builds curiosity, inspires puzzled laughter, and makes the game that follows more intriguing for all the suspense.]

Ask all your learners to stand up, and have them start wringing their hands and shifting from foot to foot. Tell them to keep doing this as they talk out loud about how they got to the workshop today. Let them continue for about 30 seconds, then ask them to stop.

Now ask them to bring their arms down and their heads up, and to stand still with their weight distributed equally on both feet. Have them take three deep, slow breaths, *focus on their bodies,* and begin talking again, this time more slowly. Give them another 30 seconds or so.

Briefly ask them what differences they noticed between the first experience and the second. [*Note:* They will almost certainly find that their bodies dictated, at least to some degree, how they spoke.] Tell them they've just practiced the Not-So-Secret Relaxation Secret, one that every seasoned speaker practices: *If you act as if you are relaxed, you become more so.* Ask how many knew that. [Show of hands.] Thank the hand-raisers for being so patient with such elementary stuff, and then invite everyone to sit down.

HOW TO PLAY THIS GAME

STAGE 1:

1. Give two 3 × 5-inch index cards to each of your learners, and have them write down one thing they happen to know a lot about on each card. (They don't need to write about their topic of expertise, just write what the topic is.)

2. Now tell them they are going to speak for one minute, on camera, about one of the two subjects they wrote about on their cards. (Reassure anxious learners by saying they will do

this again at the end of the activity, so they should consider this first taping a throwaway.)

3. One by one, bring your learners to the front, have them use the Not-So-Secret Relaxation Secret they just practiced, then videotape the one-minute speech.

4. When everyone has taken a turn, shut off the camera. Tell the group they will look at these speeches at the end of the activity. For now, they're going to add onto the Not-So-Secret Relaxation Secret, with a secret many professional speakers *don't* practice: Have a little gosh-darned fun!

STAGE 2:

1. Divide learners into pairs by having them walk around the room and find someone whose clothes have at least one color in common with their own. (*Note:* If you have any left-outs, instruct them to look at each other to see if their clothes have *anything* in common. A learner will often enjoy saying, "We're both *wearing* clothes!" Be sure to laugh at this one no matter how many times you hear it.)

2. Invite a volunteer up to the front of the room with you, to demonstrate Gibberish Experts. Your volunteer will pretend to be a noted authority on whatever subject the class chooses, and to answer all its questions. The good news is that the volunteer doesn't have to know *anything* about the topic at all! Why? Because he or she is from an overseas country called Bolinglia, and no one in the audience will be able to understand anything the volunteer says. As the volunteer speaks in Bolinglian, *you,* the trusted aid, will interpret. All that your noted authority and you have to do is *look credible.* You will do this, of course, by using the Not-So-Secret Relaxation Secret—standing still, keeping your heads up and weight evenly distributed, making eye contact, taking your time speaking, and so on. (Both of you start doing this now.)

3. Get a topic from the audience (for example, South American Land and Labor Systems), and graciously open the floor to audience questions. With each question, turn to your ex-

pert and interpret in gibberish: "Vig soya blabbif fong trakker rik?" Then allow the volunteer to hold forth: "Blabbif fonk trakker san stonkensay *darga hom*." Turn back to the audience and say something like, "Dr. Progy says the main agricultural crop is *darga hom*, a sort of cross between corn on the cob and a beet." (A tip here: It is amazingly easy to form answers if you *play off your expert's nonverbal cues*—tone of voice, facial expression, hand gestures, etc. Be sure to share this tip with your learners afterward—it will make the game *much* more fun to watch!) Take several more questions, then tell your learners it's their turn.

4. One by one, have the pairs stand before the class as Gibberish Experts. Each pair will get a topic from the audience, answer three to four questions about it, and then bow to rapt applause.

5. Now turn the camera back on. One by one, have your learners again use the Not-So-Secret Relaxation Secret (breathe, center, etc.), and videotape them speaking for one minute about the topic they wrote about on their second card.

STAGE 3:

1. Rewind the tape to the start and play back all your learners' speeches. Keep pointing out those moments when they look most relaxed. Note why that is. (Did they use the Not-So-Secret Relaxation Secret? Were they genuinely having fun?) Reinforce that, for better or worse, audiences respond as much to *the way you speak* as to *what you say.* ("You could be speaking gibberish!") Remind them to use this knowledge only for good.

DEBRIEFING QUESTIONS

- What differences did *you* notice between your first taped speech and your second? [*Note:* Usually your learners will think their second speeches look and feel more natural.] What do *you* think accounted for these differences?

- What was it like to talk nonsense—if not out-and-out gibberish—all the while conducting yourself like an expert?
- You realize you were all "phony experts." Did anyone *feel* like a phony—feel uncomfortable? Why or why not? [*Answer:* Usually your learners will find they *didn't* feel like phonies because the whole thing was in fun.] If relaxing helps you feel more comfortable even in a game, would it help you during a serious presentation?
- **KEY POINTS:** Do you think seasoned speakers remind themselves to relax before each speech? [Answer: Yes!] Do you think they remind themselves to have fun? [Answer: For many, regrettably, no.]
- What have you learned about having fun with your presentations? Can you maintain your credibility as a speaker even when having fun?

TIPS ON MAKING THIS GAME WORK WELL

When playing back the taped speeches at the end of the game, *don't* hit the pause button for your comments (or at the very least be extremely careful doing so)! Think about it: Have you ever seen yourself paused on tape at exactly the moment when you were looking your most dull-witted—mouth drooping open, one eye half shut? It's like seeing your driver's license photo up on a billboard! Try not to put your learners through this horrible experience, if only because they'll be so busy writhing they won't be able to hear your constructive commentary.

Note: Thanks to Chris Miller, Sowing Wild Arts, for inspiring this game.

OTHER TOPICS THIS GAME TEACHES

- How to Be a Naturally Funny Trainer
- Facilitation Skills

GAME 3—PILLARS

THE POINT OF THIS GAME

Truly personable speakers make it their business to **make their audience look good**. They take pains to make audience input a planned part of all their presentations. They respond positively to audience comments that are (How shall we say this?) *less than productive.* Even in the face of hostile ques-

tions, they are unfailingly respectful, assuming the questioner has at least some sincere motive.

All of this makes their listeners feel like *participants* in the presentation—that it is truly a two-way communication. (And in all but the direst of situations, isn't that what communication should be?) This in turn inspires listener buy-in, that priceless attitude that *this message is personally relevant to me.* In addition, it actually takes pressure off these speakers. They no longer have to be the originator of all wisdom in the discussion at hand! Such speakers realize something important: *There is a wealth of knowledge among their listeners, if only they are willing to tap it.* Inevitably their presentations are the richer for this realization.

This game lets your learners practice making other people's contributions work with good-natured humor. In the process, they will find that these contributions can often take them to new (and sometimes very interesting) places!

TIME NEEDED

30 minutes

MATERIALS NEEDED

A whiteboard or flip chart

A SUGGESTED FUNNY INTRODUCTION

"A teacher gave her fourth-grade students the beginning of a list of famous sayings and asked them to provide original endings for each one. Here are some examples of what they submitted [*Note:* Choose your own favorites.]:

The grass is always greener when you leave the sprinkler on.

A rolling stone plays the guitar.

No news is no newspaper.

It's better to light one candle than to waste electricity.

It's always darkest just before I open my eyes.

If you can't take the heat, don't start the fireplace.

The squeaking wheel gets annoying.

Early to bed and early to rise is first in the bathroom.

There is nothing new under the bed.

Don't count your chickens—it takes too long.

Laugh and the world laughs with you. Cry, and someone yells, "Shut up!"

"If children are capable of such intellectual gold, imagine what your adult audiences can offer! The fact is, we *all* have something interesting to contribute. It may not always fit smoothly into the topic at hand. But often, if we look below the surface, we will find a connection we didn't expect. This can add immeasurable wealth to our presentations—if only we are willing to see the gold hidden among the rocks."

HOW TO PLAY THIS GAME

1. Ask your learners for a work-related scenario involving two people. (Example: two coworkers on a project together.) Write this down on the whiteboard or flip chart.

2. Select four volunteers to do a role-play in front of the group. (If you think your learners will be shy about volunteering, see

Chapter 10, Game 1, or Chapter 9, Game 4 for ways to find people who *secretly* want to be volunteers.)

3. Have the volunteers play *Faux* Ro-Sham-Bo. They do the usual Scissors-Paper-Rock game, but the first two who make the same gesture—scissors, paper, or rock—become Persons A. The two remaining volunteers will be Persons B.

4. Persons A will be the actors in the scene, Persons B their script assistants. Persons B will stand next to their A partners, and, when tapped on the shoulder, will feed them their next lines. However, the whole scene will be improvised—no one will know what the "next line" is! So the job of Persons B will be to *come up with whatever lines they think Persons A are hoping to hear.* The job of Persons A will then be to *take whatever lines Persons B give them, and make them work as well as the lines they themselves had in mind.* Challenge your volunteers to let go of their own ideas of what would work best in the scene. After all, everyone can cling to their own ideas. The real challenge is to practice an art few speakers really master—sharing the stage!

5. Demonstrate this first yourself. Start off by saying something positive: "I really appreciate working with you, Alvin. You—" then tap one of the Persons B on the shoulder. The person will probably catch on immediately: "—are always on the same page with me." Incorporate that offering into your monologue: "—are *always* on the same page with me. In fact, I completely trust you. So—" Tap Person B again. He or she may say, "So what do you think about my presentation to the boss yesterday?" Immediately go with this: "So what do you think about my presentation to the boss yesterday? Tell me the truth. You know I'll trust your judgment completely." Tap Person B again: "Please be honest with me." Say: "*Please be honest with me. I need to know how I'm doing. ...*" Let your volunteers watch you accommodate your partner this way, then set them loose.

6. Give the volunteers 5 minutes or so to do their improvised role-play. Then, at the right moment (see Tips on Making This

Game Work Well), cut in and say, "All right! Ladies and gentlemen, let's hear it for the actors!" Lead a rousing round of applause and invite your triumphant volunteers to take their seats.

DEBRIEFING QUESTIONS

- You just watched Persons A 1) go in a certain direction, 2) solicit input from Persons B, and 3) *change direction as necessary to make that input work.* You also watched Persons B try to suggest lines they felt would not get the biggest laughs, but would *best help their partners' scenes work.* How did it feel to watch people focus on making each other's ideas work? Was it enjoyable? Did you laugh? Why? How would it have been different if they'd each tried to conduct a hilarious, one-person show?

- To Persons A: What did you have to do to change gears and accommodate Person B's lines in the scene? How did it feel to change gears? What made it easier?

- To Persons B: What did you have to do to give Persons A lines that would make things easiest for them? How did it feel when your Person A made your line work? **KEY POINT:** Did you feel more like participating?

- To all volunteers: What was it like letting go of your own idea of where the scene should go? Were you ever disappointed with the result? Were you ever pleasantly surprised?

- Was this scene more interesting and fun, or less so, because of the element of give-and-take? Why?

TIPS ON MAKING THIS GAME WORK WELL

How to end the scene: Any line that gets a healthy laugh after (or just before) the 5-minute mark is a great place to cut in! Why? Because this will ensure that your volunteers come out of it *looking good,* and the exercise ends on a high note.

Remind your volunteers that they should not try in any way to be zany, crazy, or funny. Again, the point of this game is essentially *cooperation*—the willingness to share power with someone else.

It is extremely helpful to have first played Game 1 of this chapter, Phrase Ball, with your learners. That game will acquaint them with the value of *daring to be banal*. Also useful are Game 1 from Chapter 1, Game 3 from Chapter 2, and Game 1 from Chapter 4. All of these games demonstrate beautifully how easy it is to get laughs just by *playing along with other people's ideas*.

OTHER TOPICS THIS GAME TEACHES

- Team Building
- Creative Problem Solving
- How to Be a Naturally Funny Trainer

GAME 4—WHO CARES?

THE POINT OF THIS GAME

Truly personable speakers **genuinely feel their message**. No matter how many times they have delivered their presentation, it always sounds fresh. Even speeches that are memorized (or even read) seem conversational.

How do these speakers accomplish this feat? By using a similar technique to one regularly employed by journalists: constantly asking themselves, as they deliver their message, *"So what?"*

It is not enough to tell the world the rain forests are disappearing. The world will want to know: What does this mean? Why is it a problem? How will it personally affect me? In short, Why should I care?

This game will almost certainly make some of your learners feel uncomfortable (at least in the beginning). But as they rise to the challenge of addressing the *So What*, they will develop a vital skill for presenting their message with exceptional animation and sincerity.

TIME NEEDED

15–20 minutes

MATERIALS NEEDED

None

PREPARATION

Your learners will need to have three minutes of a speech prepared and memorized. If it's possible, we suggest they use a speech they have delivered many times before.

You'll need a large, open area to play this game, so push chairs and tables against the walls.

A SUGGESTED FUNNY INTRODUCTION

"I want to start by informing you of three things: 1) this game is for your own good; 2) others have played it; and 3) they all survived and are doing nicely.

"Okay. Have you ever noticed that the most effective speakers are able to create *genuine connections* with their listeners, somehow making each one feel he or she is being spoken to *personally*? In other words, they always come across as if addressing an audience of one. In this game, you will each literally deliver a three-minute speech to an audience of one—your partner. Your job: to maintain a genuine, personal connection with that person at all times.

"Sound easy? Well, maybe. Maybe not.

"See, your partner happens to be the one person on the planet the *least interested* in your message. He or she doesn't give a rat's patootie about anything you say. [Pause for uncomfortable laughter.] Yep. Don't you hate when that happens?

"And yet it *does* happen. In fact, has anyone ever seen it happen? [Invite a couple of learners to share their experience, either as speaker or audience member, when a presenter failed to connect with listeners. Such stories will add an invaluable element of relevance to this game.]

"A *big* part of your job as a speaker is to create *personal interest* in your message. And the best way to do that is for *you* to feel personally interested—and to convey that interest by speaking to your audiences from the gut.

"This game may make you a little uncomfortable at first. That's because you'll be facing the biggest challenge any speaker has: to be real. But if you want to be in the top 5 percent of speakers, you'll face this challenge.

"The good news: If you face it today, you'll do so in the company of supportive friends! Whereas if you leave it till later, you'll face it all alone at a podium in some hotel meeting room.

"With that cheerful thought in mind—everybody up!"

HOW TO PLAY THIS GAME

1. Divide your learners into pairs by having them hold up one, two, or three fingers, and then circulate around the room seeking one other person who is holding up the same number of fingers. Once in pairs, have them decide who is shorter. That will be Person A.

2. Have partners shake hands and say, "I apologize for what is to come. I really *do* think you're interesting."

3. Persons A will now deliver their three-minute speeches to Persons B. But the moment they begin to talk, Persons B must turn their backs and walk away, saying, "Who cares?"

4. Throughout this first round, Persons B must keep walking away, repeating, "So what? Who cares?" Persons A should follow, continuing their speeches unbroken. Persons A should not change a word of their message but simply use this experience to *feel* their message more strongly. Internally, they should think about why this speech is important and why Person B should care. Then they should allow—not force, but *allow*—this feeling to show in their vocal intonation, their facial expressions, and their body language.

5. Give the pairs 3 minutes, then call time.

6. Now tell the partners to switch roles: Persons B must deliver their speeches while Persons A walk away. Again, give them 3 minutes for this.

7. Have the partners apologize to each other once more, and shake hands. Then invite them to return to their seats.

156

DEBRIEFING QUESTIONS

- How did it feel to insist on being heard? Do speakers sometimes have to do this? When and why?

- What were your thoughts or feelings when you were being ignored? Did you in any way adjust your speaking style? If so, how?

- When do speakers encounter audiences that think their message is irrelevant? Why do you think this happens?

- Does it make any difference when the speaker *feels* his or her message? How?

OTHER TOPICS THIS GAME TEACHES

How to Be a Naturally Funny Trainer

GAME 5—ELEMENTARY, MY DEAR WATSONS

THE POINT OF THIS GAME

Truly personable speakers **commit to their message.**

It has been said that 80 percent of professionals suffer from Impostor Syndrome—the belief that they are neither knowledgeable or experienced enough to act as subject matter experts.* Usually this happens less because of any incompetence, and more because they have simply moved outside their comfort zones, been asked to do something they have not done before.

Surprise! This describes many speakers.

After all, how many of us, after having 1) been given the responsibility to communicate a message before a group, 2) done our research, and 3) practiced our delivery before the bedroom mirror, still live in fear that we will be found out by our audiences as (Horrors!) mere mortals—fallible human beings who don't know all answers to all questions?

This fear of being found out inhibits many otherwise solid speakers, causing them to look and sound tentative about their message. This game helps new speakers practice committing to the message so that they appear confident about the validity of their information in front of groups.

---

*For more on Imposter Syndrome—assuming you yourself have never experienced it (!)—see Pamela Gilbert, *The Eleven Commandments of Wildly Successful Women*, (MacMillan Spectrum, 1998) and *The Twelfth Commandment of Wildly Successful Women* (Chandler House Press, 1999).

(*Note:* It may seem from this citation that women suffer more from Imposter Syndrome than men. To this we can only reply: What a shocker! Nonetheless, we anticipate our male readers will find that the above sources are relevant to their circumstances.

TIME NEEDED

40 minutes

MATERIALS NEEDED

An egg timer, stopwatch, or other timing device

A SUGGESTED FUNNY INTRODUCTION

The funniest and most efficient way to introduce this game is to quickly *demonstrate* it with one learner. First, as Partner 2, you will get lots of laughs as you boldly try (and fail) to decipher Partner 1's clues. Second, demonstrating is far simpler than explaining the game. Third, by briefly *playing* the game, you will model the *principle* of the game—commitment—through your own good-natured willingness to try, try again. (For more on this, see Tips on Making This Game Work Well.)

HOW TO PLAY THIS GAME

1. Get four volunteers to form a team and to count off as Players 1, 2, 3, and 4. (*Note:* We have found it is rarely hard to find volunteers for this game, no matter who the learners are. Everyone finds this one completely intriguing.)

2. Describe the game: A murder has been committed. Player 1 will be told by the audience 1) the *occupation* of the murderer, 2) the *room* in the house in which the murder took place, and 3) the *weapon* used. Player 1 will then communicate these facts to Player 2 using only gibberish and mime (dramatic gestures, made-up language but no real words). Player 2 will then use gibberish and mime to pass along this information to Player 3 who will then do the same to Player 4. The players will have a total of 5 minutes to pass along their guesses to all four members.

3. The audience will have two jobs. Their first task will be to call out an occupation, a room, and a murder weapon for Player 1. Advise the audience that the murder weapon need not be

a typical weapon. For instance, the audience could suggest the murderer used a giant salami, a blackboard, a fishing pole, anything at all. The audience's second job will be to signal to each player when they have made a correct guess through enthusiastic applause.

4. Ask Players 2, 3, and 4 to stand facing the wall with their fingers in their ears and quietly hum "Happy Birthday" to themselves. (This is the cheap, low-tech version of a soundproof room.) While they are humming, Player I should ask the audience to name an occupation, a room, and a murder weapon. (*Note:* The audience members are likely to all call out different things at once; advise Player I to take the first suggestion he or she hears.)

5. When Player I has gotten the three items, start the timer. Player I must now tap Player 2 on the shoulder, run with him or her to the center of the room, and begin miming the information. As they play, constantly remind them: "Three minutes left. Two minutes. One minute." (See Tips on Making This Game Work Well.)

6. Once Player 2 has figured out all three pieces of information, he or she must mime holding or using the murder weapon, "kill" Player I, then run to Player 3 and begin passing on the information, again through mime and gibberish. When Player 3 has got it, he or she must "kill" Player 2, grab Player 4, and carry on until Player 4 gets it, or the 5-minute timer rings. *Inform the team that it is more important to get through all the players than to get all the facts correct.*

7. When the timer goes off, quiz Player 4: "What was the occupation? The room? The weapon?" No matter how flummoxed Player 4 is, he or she must *convey complete confidence* while answering each question. (*Note:* As you will already have demonstrated, this will get huge laughs from the audience.) Lead a round of applause for the team, and have them sit down.

8. Bring up a second and third team if you have time, and repeat the process with a new occupation, room, and murder weapon.

DEBRIEFING QUESTIONS

- The point of this game was not to teach you to *feign knowledge*, but to *stop dwelling on your lack of knowledge*. If you don't realize this by now, it's time you did: Even the most experienced, competent people get insecure—sometimes even terrified—about their "insufficient knowledge" when facing new or challenging situations! But who that has ever accomplished anything had full information at the outset?

- What are some dangers of Impostor Syndrome? [Possible answers: needlessly undermining audience confidence in your message; inspiring excessive questioning; creating unnecessary tension; slowing progress.]

- To the players: How did it feel to play with confidence—to *claim expertise* even when you didn't always know what the heck was going on? Did it help that this was just a game?

- What about claiming expertise in real life? Is that appropriate when you aren't a world authority on your subject? [Answer: Most people aren't world authorities. Yet we need to get our information from *someone*. There is no reason to apologize for not having all the answers to all the questions.]

- What should you do when you don't have an answer to an audience question? Apologize and slink off the stage? [Answer: Of course not. But at the same time, don't pretend to know what you don't know! Some solutions: suggest resources; throw the question open to audience discussion; offer what answers you *do* have in a positive, confident manner, and suggest that there may be others.]

- What was it like to watch the players go for it—take their ideas and run with them, and damn the torpedoes?

This game is not complicated, but describing it is! For this reason, *we strongly suggest that you play the game yourself before attempting to demonstrate and lead it.* Consider trying it out with another trainer or some other colleague. If you have kids over the age of 9, play the game with them. They will love it, and interestingly enough, kids seem to be naturals at playing this game well!)

When demonstrating the game, be sure to model the necessary hot-dogging spirit. Each time you have even a vague idea what your partner is talking about, give a knowing "Aaaaah!" and unhesitatingly mimic your "understanding." Example: Suppose the murderer's occupation is baker. Your partner might first mime being hungry, rubbing his or her stomach and saying, "Mmmmm, glabba hum." You might decide they have a stomach ache, and take this to mean the occupation is doctor. Rather than wait for confirmation, you should unhesitatingly open up a bottle of pills and hand two to your partner: "Aaaaah! Farga preebo." Your partner will shake his or her head, and perhaps mime slicing bread: *"Glabba, glabba!"* You might then think the occupation is short-order cook, take the knife away from your partner, and make a club sandwich: "Aaaah, *glabba.*" Your partner will again shake his or her head, and mime taking a cake out of the oven: "Plubf!" You might finally catch on—"Aaaaah, *plubf!*"— and begin frosting the cake.

When quizzing Partners 4 at the end, you will find that some of their guesses are correct. Lead applause for this. When they are way off on their guesses, the proper response from you is always: "Oh, *so* close!" Then tell them what the real answer was.

Warning: It is typical for teams (at least those new to this game) to spend the entire 5 minutes on Player 2, and never get to Players 3 or 4—don't let them! This is usually because Player 2 doesn't want to be wrong in guessing. It is also the reason this game is so good for helping people to let go of the Impostor Syndrome. In this case, the more they commit to their ideas, right or wrong, the more audiences howl! Keep pushing them to move fast; if a partner can't figure out one clue, have him or her move on to the next one.

OTHER TOPICS THIS GAME TEACHES

- Creative Problem Solving
- How to Be a Naturally Funny Trainer

7

Five Games to Increase Emotional Intelligence

GAME 1—EMOTIONAL CONTAGION

THE POINT OF THIS GAME

People with high levels of emotional intelligence **recognize
how emotions affect our interactions with others**. In
fact, as anyone who works in
close contact with others can at-
test, strong emotions, especially
negative emotions, can be caught
and passed on much like a virus.
This short game illustrates this
phenomenon quickly and effectively.

TIME NEEDED

Approximately 10 minutes (best played with groups of more
than 20 people)

MATERIALS NEEDED

None

A SUGGESTED FUNNY INTRODUCTION

"Has anyone ever met a real *wet blanket*? You know, the person
who has a hundred good reasons why things will never work—
who is so depressing, he or she could make *Richard Simmons* eat
a whole carton of Rocky Road in one sitting? [Show of hands,
groans, venting laughter.] And not just Richard. Ever notice how
that one negative person can zap the morale of an entire *room-

ful of people? [More groans.] Does one *cheerful* person have the same power over a roomful of wet blankets? No way!

"Why *is* that? Ever wonder?

"Well, psychologist Martin Seligman* says we may be genetically programmed toward negativity. He reminds us that our most recent evolutionary ancestors lived during the Pleistocene period—a hundred-thousand-year age of climactic upheaval. Ice ages, heat waves, floods, droughts, famine. … A little more stressful than someone's car alarm waking you up in the middle of the night, wouldn't you say?

"Dr. Seligman suggests that the people who survived may have done so because they were pessimists! They didn't *expect* good times to last. They worried all the time about a bleak future. Let's face it, what if every time the weather was nice they'd said, "I have a hunch it'll stay this way. Think I'll just kick back and grab some rays. I can always root for grubs tomorrow." That may not have been the best survival strategy for the times.

"In other words, we may all be descendants of … worry warts! We're genetically wired to respond to negativity. Isn't that good news?

"Let's do an exercise right now that can show us how easy it is to become infected by each other's negative emotions. Everybody up!"

HOW TO PLAY THIS GAME

1. The object of this game will be to spread an emotion through the room via the act of winking. One person will be designated as Ground Zero Winker. This person's task will be to infect three other people in the room with irritability. Anyone who gets winked at will consider himself or herself infected with irritability. Once infected, a learner's task will be to wink at three other people to infect them. When an infected person has winked at three people, he or she will continue to mill around but should stop winking.

*Author of *Learned Optimism* (New York, Knopf, 1991), among many other books.

2. To be begin the game, ask the learners to stand in a circle with their eyes closed.

3. Walk around the outside of the circle several times and lightly tap one learner on the back. This person will be the Ground Zero Winker.

4. Ask the learners to open their eyes and to mill around the room, as if at a cocktail party. Learners can introduce themselves, shake hands, and engage in light conversation while they interact with as many people as possible.

5. Call time after 5 minutes and ask the learners to sit down.

6. Ask for the first infected person (Ground Zero Winker) to stand and to remain standing.

7. Ask the three people who were infected by this person to stand.

8. Ask that the learners who were infected by these three people stand.

9. Continue exponentially until most if not all learners are standing. (*Note:* It will only take a few minutes for a group as large as 60 people to be infected.)

10. Let the visual sink in and then suggest that anyone who really does feel irritated at this point can be seated. Then state that *everyone*, even if they're feeling perky, can have a seat.

ROUND 2 (optional)

1. Tell the learners that an antidote to irritability has been found and that this antidote is spread through sincere and warm smiles. Because this group is now so riddled with irritability, it is imperative that the group get this antidote soon.

2. Ask the group to rise again and stand in a circle with their eyes closed. Advise them that you will choose a learner to act as Ground Zero Smiler, who will provide the antidote to irritability by smiling at three people. Anyone who gets smiled at should, in turn, smile at three more people.

3. Walk around the outside of the group, but do not touch any-one on the back. Simply say "Go" at some point, as if you had designated someone to be Ground Zero Smiler.

4. Let the group mill around for 3 minutes. Call time and ask all to be seated.

5. Ask for the learners who received the smiling antidote to raise their hands.

6. Ask the group to point to the person they thought was the Ground Zero Smiler. You may find fingers pointing in many different directions.

7. Tell the group that, actually, science has not yet developed a good antidote to irritability and there was no Ground Zero Smiler. In fact, sneaky trainer that you are, you simply admin-istered a placebo, and the group was cured simply because they *expected* to be cured.

DEBRIEFING QUESTIONS

- Ask the learners to describe what happened in this round. Did anyone get smiled at? Did anyone just have to smile?

- Recall the first round. How did it feel to be infected with irri-tability? What thoughts or feelings did you have?

- Did anyone begin to truly feel irritated after being infected? Did you notice any changes in your nonverbal or verbal be-haviors that were consistent with being irritable?

- Did anyone try to avoid being infected? How?

- Were your reactions different when smiles were being spread?

- In this game, your expectation that you were going to be smiled at actually induced you to get and give smiles. How do your expectations in real life influence your attitudes and be-havior? How might you get self-fulfilling behaviors?

- How does emotional contagion play out in real life at your workplace? What typically happens when someone in your of-

170

fice is in a bad mood? How do people's emotions affect others?

- How do your moods affect your colleagues?
- What emotions seem to have the most impact on a team's performance? On you personally?
- What might be the business impact of a workplace filled with negative emotions?
- How can you avoid being infected with a negative emotion in real life? What can you do to build up your own immunity and resiliency?

OTHER TOPICS THIS GAME TEACHES

- Communication Skills
- Team Building
- Reducing Workplace Negativity
- Dealing with Stress

GAME 2—AS THE COMPANY TURNS

THE POINT OF THIS GAME

People with high levels of emotional intelligence **accurately observe and interpret the verbal and nonverbal behaviors of others**. This ability helps the emotionally intelligent person to adapt to the other person's needs and style. This game will help your learners practice their observation and assessment skills.

TIME NEEDED

45–50 minutes

MATERIALS NEEDED

- A Character Background sheet for each team, preferably reproduced on flip chart paper (See handouts.)
- As the Company Turns Observation Worksheet (See handouts.)
- Highway signs (See handouts.)

PREPARATION

Put the following gender-neutral names on flip chart paper: Terry, Chris, Alex, Robin, Sandy, Kyle, Pat, Kim.

A SUGGESTED FUNNY INTRODUCTION

Use the highway signs on the handout sheet at the end of this game to demonstrate how some people misread signs. For example, tell them one person thought the No U-Turn sign meant "Do not bend over." Someone else thought the Slippery Roads sign meant "Drunk driving allowed." The School Crosswalk sign has been misread as "Purse snatching in progress," and Keep Right as "Dodge bullet." Soberly tell your learners you expect better of their observation and interpretation skills.

HOW TO PLAY THIS GAME

1. Choose three people to act as judges. Divide the rest of your learners into two teams.

2. Give each team a Character Background sheet on flip chart paper. This sheet will serve as a guide to help the teams create a fictional character. The character should not be based on any real person at the company, but can be a kind of composite figure. Encourage the teams to create a person who embodies traits typical to employees at their workplace, but in a slightly exaggerated form. Each team should choose a gender-neutral name from the list you have posted.

3. Give the teams 10 minutes to complete all the categories in the Character Background sheet.

4. After 10 minutes, tell the teams to choose a learner who will play this character in a soap opera drama called "As the Company Turns." The scene will take place between two workers of the company who are stuck in the elevator together.

5. Describe how the game will be played: The two learners representing their team's characters will go to the front of the room. They will be their characters for a 5- to 10-minute role-play. The players have two goals during the roleplay. The first is to reveal their characters' nature during the course of the role-play. The second goal is to uncover traits of the other character, so that their team members can develop an accurate profile.

6. Give the teams 5 to 10 minutes prior to the role-play to offer suggestions to their players about how to depict their characters' traits during the role-play. For example, to indicate that the character is an impatient female executive, a player might tap her feet, look at her watch, and complain that the heels of one of her expensive Italian shoes broke on the way from her company parking spot. The only rule is that the player cannot literally describe himself or herself during the role-play. A player cannot simply say, "I'm a 34-year-old guy working in sales." The person's character needs to be revealed through a natural-sounding dialogue with the other character. This dialogue, however, can consist of questions such as: "So where are you on your way to?" or "I like what you're wearing, what's that called?"

7. During the role-play, learners need to watch their opposing team's representative closely. Just as in charades, the objective is to correctly identify who this character is.

8. Begin the role-play. "It is 8:55 a.m. As our drama opens, two workers from our company are on the way up in the elevator. Suddenly the elevator shudders, there is a loud grinding noise, and the elevator jolts to a stop. Let's see what happens next ..."

9. If the players get stuck at any point, they can ask their teammates for suggestions on what to say or ask next. You can also intervene at any time to play a maintenance person on the elevator telephone or an irate boss asking a subordinate a question.

10. As the learners watch the role play, they should record their personal observations and guesses on their observation worksheets. Remember that they are observing the opposing team's character.

11. When the role-play is over, the learners will meet back with their original teams. Their task is now to reach a consensus decision regarding the traits the opposing team player was trying to portray. They should record the team's answers in the column indicated on the observation worksheets.

12. Ask each team to reveal its guesses about the opposing team's character. ("We think your character was feeling depressed.") After each guess, the other team reveals its original profile.

13. The three judges will determine whether a team was close enough to merit points. Teams receive points for the following:

   • 2 points for each correct assessment they make about the opposing team's character

   • 3 points for any correct answer on a bonus question

DEBRIEFING QUESTIONS

• Would you want to work with these characters? What did they say or do to influence your opinion?

• How did the characters reveal their values or beliefs? How do people reveal themselves in real life?

• How aware would you say you normally are to the clues people give about themselves? What gets in the way of accurately observing others?

• What assumptions did you make? Why? How does generalizing help or hinder our ability to read others in real life?

• How accurate were you personally about the character's traits compared to the rest of your team? Did you get talked out of a correct answer? What were your thoughts and intentions in conceding to the rest of the group? [Note that the ability to collaborate is an important sign of emotional intelligence, but so is the ability to stand by one's own insights and opinions.]

• Note that the two players asked each other questions to help get to know each other. What kinds of questions could you ask in real life to increase your understanding of others? How important would this be in working with a new team, in negotiating a contract, in asking for feedback on your performance, and so on?

- Think of your closest colleague at work. If you were to complete a character background sheet on this person, how many of the questions could you answer? Do you know this person's stated ambition as well as his or her secret ambition?

- How well would you be able to answer these questions about someone you do not like at work? Would your relationship with this person change if you knew more about her or him? Why do we resist getting to know some people (usually people we dislike)? What are the possible business consequences of this resistance?

- If you were playing one of the characters in the role-play, what were you thinking and feeling during the role-play? What questions were most effective in helping your partner to reveal himself or herself? How did this role-play mirror your real-life experiences in learning about someone?

TIPS ON MAKING THIS GAME WORK WELL

You may want to instruct your three judges to act as process observers, watching how team members communicate with each other. Judges can then be asked to share their observations during the de-briefing. Specifically, judges should make note of how effectively group members communicated their ideas and listened to each other's suggestions.

OTHER TOPICS THIS GAME TEACHES

- Dealing with Difficult People
- Team Building
- Communication Skills

HIGHWAY SIGNS SAMPLES

SIGN 1:

SIGN 2:

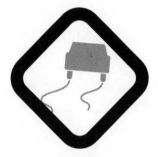

SIGN 3:

SIGN 4:

AS THE COMPANY TURNS
CHARACTER BACKGROUND SHEET

(Note: This sheet should be reproduced on flip chart paper for each team.)

Describe Your Character's:

Gender

Job title

Status at work

Most intense feeling at this moment

Stated ambition

Favorite task at work

Bonus Questions:

Hidden fear

Secret ambition

AS THE COMPANY TURNS
OBSERVATION WORKSHEET

Directions: Watch the role-play and observe the opposing team's player closely. Guess this character's profile based on his or her verbal and non-verbal behavior.

	Your Guess	Team's Decision
What is this character's:		
Gender		
Job title		
Status at work		
Most intense feeling at this moment		
Stated ambition		
Favorite task at work		
BONUS QUESTIONS:		
* Hidden fear		
* Secret ambition		

GAME 3—SELLING SNOW PLOWS TO HAWAIIANS

THE POINT OF THIS GAME

People who are emotionally intelligent are able to **communicate clear and convincing messages** that engender openness and receptivity among their listeners. This game will help learners practice their skills at persuasiveness and empathy in the most difficult of all situations: selling the unsellable.

TIME NEEDED

30 minutes

MATERIALS NEEDED

• Snow Plows to Hawaiians cards. Write the following phrases on individual index cards:

Golf clubs to hospital administrators

Lawn chairs to airlines

Hot dog buns to vegetarians

Bubble gum to the Teachers Association

Typewriters to a high-tech company

Lie detector test to staff at a political party headquarters

Passes to Graceland for the cast of the Metropolitan Opera

Lawn mowers to apartment dwellers

Vitamins to morticians

Cigarettes to athletes

A SUGGESTED FUNNY INTRODUCTION

"Some people are a little unclear on the concept when it comes to selling their products. Ever hear about the Midwest company that advertised its product as 'Good as any, better than some'? One Chicago radio station has this as its slogan: 'Of all the radio stations in Chicago, we're one of them.' And the advertisement for a musical comedy once read, 'You'll laugh till you stop.'

"It's safe to say that if you want to be persuasive, you need to work a little harder to convey the WIIFM—What's In It For Me?—to your listeners. Let's practice that right now. ..."

HOW TO PLAY THIS GAME

1. Discuss a key concept of emotional intelligence: the ability to understand others' perspectives and to align one's own goals with the values and goals of the other person. People who excel at this ability successfully move and influence others. They could, indeed, sell snow plows to Hawaiians.

2. Tell the learners they are all hot-shot members of a cutting-edge advertising company. This is a firm known for taking on tough clients and unusual products.

3. Divide the learners into triads and give each group a Snow Plows to Hawaiians card. Each card names a product and a specific population this item is to be sold to. The problem is that on the surface, it does not look as if this population needs this particular item. In fact, on the surface, it looks as if this population would reject this product completely. The challenge for each group, therefore, is to sell the unsellable.

4. Each group is to come up with a one-minute radio advertisement that will sell its item to the population described. The commercial should illustrate three points:

   a. how the item will make life better for this population;

   b. how this population could use the item in creative and useful ways; and

181

c. how the item matches this population's unique goals and values.

5. Give the small groups 10 to 15 minutes. The groups should first discuss the points step 4 listed and then write a one-minute advertising piece that addresses those points in a compelling and persuasive manner.

6. Each group will deliver the radio ad to the rest of the learners as if they were the target population. The learners should listen to the ad, putting themselves in the mind-set of this population. The learners will rate the success of the ad on how well it matched the product to their needs. Learners will vote by holding up from one to five fingers, with five fingers indicating that this ad would persuade them to buy this item and one finger indicating that they would laugh the salesperson out of the room.

7. Compare scores, congratulate the winning team, and lead the applause.

DEBRIEFING QUESTIONS

- In this activity, you were twice asked to adopt another's perspective. The first time was by putting yourself in your population's shoes and seeing your product through their eyes. The second was when you were listening to the radio ad from the perspective of a different target group. What did you do in order to see the world from another's perspective? How hard or easy was it for you?

- How hard or easy is it to understand someone else's perspective in real life? How might empathy change your relationships with colleagues, bosses, and clients?

- What beliefs might you have to give up to empathize with people you disagree with?

- What strategies did your team use to sell this item? What did you imagine about the needs, thoughts, or values of your target population?

- Have you been in situations in which you believed your goals and the goals of the other person did not match? How might the skills you practiced in this activity have helped in those situations? What could you do differently if you were faced with a similar situation in the future?

OTHER TOPICS THIS GAME TEACHES

- Communication Skills
- Reducing Workplace Negativity
- Values

GAME 4—TAKE ME ... PLEASE

THE POINT OF THIS GAME

Emotionally intelligent people can **identify their own and others' strengths and limits**. This game 1) allows learners to examine how their personal qualities contribute to and hinder group functioning, 2) increases their awareness of other's strengths and lets them practice their influencing skills, and 3) provides an opportunity for them to give each other feedback. (Quite a wallop for one little game, huh? Please, hold your applause ...)

Note: This game will work best with a group in which the members know each other fairly well.

TIME NEEDED

40–60 minutes, depending on the size of the group

MATERIALS NEEDED

- Three blank index cards per learner
- Team Role Descriptions sheet (see handout)

A SUGGESTED FUNNY INTRODUCTION

"Recall a meeting from hell where you might not have been, well, at your *best*. Perhaps you were a bit impatient with a slow talker. Perhaps you *were* the slow talker. Maybe you waited till the meeting was almost over to bring up a critical issue. Maybe you yelled at someone who really, really deserved it. But what your colleagues don't understand about you is that your intentions are pure. You wanted to *help* the meeting. If only your colleagues could *appreciate* your noble qualities."

HOW TO PLAY THIS GAME

1. Distribute the index cards and Team Role Description sheets to learners.

2. Ask the learners to read over the Team Role Descriptions sheet and circle the three roles that best describe them. Instruct them to place a star next to the role that is closest to how they see themselves acting in a group.

3. Ask the learners to write their selected qualities on the index cards. (One quality per card.)

4. Collect all the cards from the learners and shuffle them thoroughly.

5. Redistribute the cards, giving each learner three new cards.

6. Ask the learners to read their new cards. Their task is to get back their original three roles (not necessarily their original cards), or end up with three cards they can live with. Learners do this by trading cards. In order to get rid of a role, a learner will approach someone else and propose a trade. It is in a learner's best interest to show the positive attributes of this role and how it fits the other person's typical behavior. Learners do not necessarily have to trade a card for a card. A learner could presumably have no cards at a given moment in this activity, or could be holding five or six. The key, however is to "sell" the role you do not want and seek the roles you do want.

7. Give the group 10 minutes for trading. Call time and ask the learners to sit in a circle.

8. Ask the learners to retrieve their Team Role Descriptions sheets.

185

9. Ask who got all three roles back? Who got *most* of their roles? Who gave up on their roles and just kept whatever they ended up with?

10. Optional activity [*Note:* If you are working with people who do not know each other well, you may want to skip this step]: Tell the learners that they are now going to enter into the psychic portion of the activity. Go around the circle and ask the group to guess which role each person chose as the one that best resembled them. Allow 1 to 2 minutes of guessing time before asking the learner to reveal the chosen role.

DEBRIEFING QUESTIONS

- Did you generally see the roles you chose as strengths or weaknesses? Could these roles provided be both a personal strength and a limitation? Under what circumstances do these change?

- There is a truism that suggests that we judge others by their actions, but ourselves by our intentions. How does this truism relate to this game and to how we behave at meetings?

- What do you wish people understood about your intentions at meetings?

- What do you wish you understood about others' intentions at meetings?

- How successful were you at finding people who would accept the cards you held? How accurate were you? What did you do or say to persuade someone who might have been hesitant?

- What was it like to reframe a role you might actually find annoying in a positive way in order to sell it?

- How might your attitudes toward your colleagues change if you could maintain this reframed perspective? How might your behavior change? How might your meetings and teamwork improve?

- Was anyone surprised at how others perceived him or her? Why might others see you differently from the way you see yourself? Based on the feedback you received, is there anything you would like to change about your behavior?
- What insights about team roles did this game suggest to you? How will these insights change your appreciation of others?

OTHER TOPICS THIS GAME TEACHES

- Conflict and Negotiation
- Dealing with Difficult People
- Leadership Skills
- Reducing Workplace Negativity
- Personality Inventory
- Team Building
- Values

TEAM ROLE DESCRIPTIONS

Directions: Check the three roles that best describe your behavior in a team or group meeting. Next, place a star next to the one role that most resembles you.

❑ **Initiator:** Suggests new ideas, gets meeting started

❑ **Information Seeker:** Seeks facts, information to help group come to a decision

❑ **Diplomat:** Builds alliances, negotiates for agreement

❑ **Conductor:** Helps move flow of information

❑ **Judge:** Listens and evaluates

❑ **Harmonizer:** Helps resolve conflicts

❑ **Task-focused:** Prods group to complete task

❑ **Challenger:** Confronts accepted ideas, provokes for new ideas

❑ **Supporter:** Supports group member's ideas

❑ **Clarifier:** Interprets ideas, clears up confusion

❑ **Expert:** Provides advice, facts, knowledge members may not have

❑ **Influencer:** Persuades others to support ideas, projects

GAME 5—THE IDEAL WORKPLACE

THE POINT OF THIS GAME

People who are emotionally intelligent **balance their attention to tasks and relationships**. This game helps learners examine the skills of collaboration and cooperation.

TIME NEEDED

20–30 minutes

MATERIALS NEEDED

- Flip chart paper for each small group
- Package of colored markers for each small group

A SUGGESTED FUNNY INTRODUCTION

"Who has ever been at a meeting that was like the Tower of Babel—everybody talking at once till you want to scream, '*Shut up*'? Well ... you won't feel that way in *this* game. Let's get started. ...''

HOW TO PLAY THIS GAME

1. Divide the learners into groups of 4 to 6. Give each group a piece of flip chart paper and markers. Encourage the groups to sit on the floor or to gather in a circle around a central table for this activity.

2. Tell the groups that their dream has come true: The office where they now work will be completely redone. No expense will be spared in making it the most efficient, com-

189

fortable and up-to-date workplace. And best of all, the architect of this project wants input from the workers about how they want their new building to look.

3. Each small group is to sketch a diagram, floor plan, or building blueprints for the new office. The sketches can use any perspective and can be as detailed as they like. The architect promises to review all their ideas. The architect had only one stipulation in how they come up with their group sketch: To encourage all group members to participate freely, the groups must work in complete silence. Learners may not talk to their fellow group members to plan or actually sketch out their design.

4. Give the groups 10 minutes to draw their ideal workplace.

5. Post the drawings as in an art gallery and have each group explain its ideas to the rest of the learners.

DEBRIEFING QUESTIONS

- What were common themes in these ideal workplaces? How do these themes reflect your values?
- How did you end up communicating your ideas to your teammates? How accurate were you in decoding what your teammates meant?
- What nonverbal clues became important?
- How would your final product be different if you had been able to talk? Would the level or quality of your participation have been different if you had been able to talk?
- Did someone on your team emerge as the leader? How did the person do that?
- Did someone on your team serve as a facilitator—encouraging participation from others or mediating conflicts? How did the person do that?
- In real life, what behaviors help a team reach its goals? What kind of internal competencies does this suggest an individual needs to be a good team player?

- What could you do differently to enhance your ability to collaborate with others? How could you use nonverbal communication more effectively?

OTHER TOPICS THIS GAME TEACHES

- Team Building
- Leadership Skills
- Communication Skills
- Reducing Workplace Negativity

8

Five Games to Reduce Workplace Negativity

The games in this chapter use humor and playfulness to help work teams identify and change negative workplace norms. Because these games build sequentially, they should be played in the order presented. Each game represents one step in a five-part process. By following these games one by one your group will 1) identify the negative behaviors that have become entrenched within the group, and 2) take systematic steps to replace these behaviors with positive ones.*

Note that after Game 1, your learners will break into two teams, playing the rest of the games in competition. You may want to purchase small candies to give to the team players as "fabulous prizes."

We also suggest that you refer to other games in this book (see especially Chapters 4, 5, and 6) to help your learners become more adept in resisting the pull of negativity.

*For a quick overview of workplace norms, see Robert F. Allen and Saul Pilnick, "Confronting the Shadow Organization: How to Detect and Defeat Negative Norms," *Organizational Dynamics*, Spring, 1973. For more detailed reading, see Robert F. Allen, Charlotte Kraft, Judd Allen, and Barry Letner, *The Organizational Unconscious: How to Create the Corporate Culture You Want and Need*, (Healthyculture.com. 1987).

GAME 1—WHO STARTED IT?

THE POINT OF THIS GAME

Before any group can change its norms, the group members must agree to **abstain from the blame game**. The members must acknowledge the fact that *everyone is to some extent responsible for group behavior*—
that no one person is at fault. This game graphically illustrates how group behavior can take on a life of its own.

TIME NEEDED

15 minutes

MATERIALS NEEDED

None

A SUGGESTED FUNNY INTRODUCTION

"How many have ever found yourselves behaving in ways you *yourselves* don't believe in? You know, gossiping or buttering up, doing that kind of thing, just because that's the way things were done in your group? [Show of hands. *Note:* Don't expect to see many. Few of your learners will consider themselves capable of such moral bankruptcy. Look surprised.] *Really?* I'm the only one?

"Okay, how many here are sick and tired of gossip and backbiting at work? [Show of hands.] Ohhh ... So when someone comes up to *you* with some really great dirt, *you* say, 'No, no, do not speak! My ears are sealed—get thee hence!' [This will *definitely* get a laugh.]

"You know, group dynamics are such that we often feel pressured to say and do things that will help us *fit in*. And that creates pressure for others, who also try to say and do these things, which creates pressure for us again, and so on and so on. ... After awhile, it's irrelevant who *started* it; everybody's making everybody *keep doing it!* Let's see an example of this group dynamic. Everybody up. ...''

HOW TO PLAY THIS GAME

1. Have your learners stand in a circle. Start things off by pointing at anyone across from you in the circle. Keep pointing. That person must now point to someone else across the circle, who then must point to another person, who must do likewise, etc., etc. *Tell them no one must point at anyone who is already pointing at someone else.* Carry on until everyone is pointing at someone, with no two people pointing at the same person. You may then all stop pointing (and apologize to each other for having been so rude as to do it at all).

2. Now tell everyone to fix their eyes on the person they just pointed at. Tell them it is their job to keep watching that person. That person is the Role Model.

3. Learners have one job: They are to watch their Role Models closely and copy those people's actions. Ask your learners to stand perfectly still. The only time they may move is if their Role Models move. In fact if the Role Model does *anything*—coughs, twitches a finger, anything at all—the learner must repeat that motion once, and then be still again (unless, of course, the Role Model moves another time).

4. Start the game, and let it go for about 5 minutes. What will happen is that small movements will occur here and there. Anytime one does, it will be repeated around the circle endlessly (and usually exaggerated with each repetition). In the end, everyone in the circle should be wagging their heads,

moving their arms, scrunching their faces, coughing, giggling, and generally acting like a bunch of nuts!

DEBRIEFING QUESTIONS

- What just happened? We were supposed to stand *still.*
- How many don't know who started some of the movements? [Let your learners argue about when this or that move originated. In fact, there should be lots of argument about "who started what" during the debriefing.]
- How many knew it was *your* Role Model who started a given movement? [*Note:* Sometimes a learner can state confidently, "Charley started the nose twitch." Ask Charley: "Are you surprised to learn that you're the one who started that? Were you aware of moving?"]
- **KEY POINT:** Did it matter who started anything, once everybody else adopted it?
- How did this game model what your group does in real life? How do you play the "who started it" game at work? What are the costs of playing this game? How important is it to you personally to stop participating in this negative cycle? What would you be willing to do to change this norm?

OTHER TOPICS THIS GAME TEACHES

- Emotional Intelligence
- Icebreaker
- Team Building

GAME 2—NAME THAT NORM!

THE POINT OF THIS GAME

It's time for your learners to **get honest about naming the negative norms** in their work environment. This task makes many groups uneasy (even after they've all agreed not to finger-point). This game will help your learners to identify the norms that influence their group. Being

able to honestly name these norms is the first step toward changing them. The format of this game offers your learners a way to take their *subject* seriously, but *themselves* lightly.

TIME NEEDED

30–40 minutes, depending on the number of norms you choose to address

MATERIALS NEEDED

- A Group Norms Sheet for each learner (see handout)
- Lots of 8½ × 11-inch paper
- A flip chart
- A stop watch or watch with a second hand

PREPARATION

Divide learners into two teams who will compete with each other in this and the next three games. One way to form teams is to have those whose birthdays fall before February 29th (leap year, of course) stand on the left side of the room, and those whose birthdays come after stand on the right. (If the two teams vary widely in size, find a few people from the bigger team whose birthdays are closest to the 29th, and move them over to the other team.)

A SUGGESTED FUNNY INTRODUCTION

"For the duration of this session, you will all be competing to win *fabulous prizes!* No, I can't divulge what they are, but let me tell you, they are plenty fabulous—no expense has been spared. So it's time to get lean and mean: Turn to your fellow team members right now and say, 'We *are* the winning team!' [Let them do this.]

"And now your first mission, should you choose to accept it, is to come up with a name for your team, so I don't have to call you 'You Guys.' You have one minute—go!"

[At the end of the minute, let them share their team names. Be sure to laugh if they use humor, which they almost certainly will. Write the team names on two separate sheets of flip chart paper taped side by side on the wall. These will be the teams' scoreboards. Then tell your learners:]

"Throughout the rest of the day, you will win points for doing well in the activities. But you will *also* get *bonus* points, for things like *laughs*—specifically, one, two, or three points, depending on how big the laugh is. (By the way—the laughs have to come from *the other team.* That's right, no laughing uproariously at your own jokes just to beef up your score!) You will also get five points for any act of *creativity*, however I define that. Why do *I* get to define what is creative, you ask? Because I am the Big Kahuna, of course.

"Now, without any further ado ... let the games begin!"

HOW TO PLAY THIS GAME

1. This game is played like Charades.

   Take a moment to describe the term *norms* for your learners. The word *norms* refers to behavioral rules that govern how people act in a group. Put another way, norms are "how we do things around here." In general, group norms are unquestioned (and often unstated). New members of a group learn the norms through observation or trial and error.

2. Give each learner a copy of the Group Norms Sheet handout. Ask the teams to choose two or three of the norms they see as having the most negative impact on their workplace. In other words, they should choose those norms that, if improved, would make the biggest difference in their quality of life at work. (*Note:* You can also ask the teams to use all of the categories.)

3. Under each category, the teams must now describe *specific* behaviors in which, in their observation, *they and others regularly engage at work.* Have them do this by writing, "What do *most of us around here* do when ..." and then finish the question.* The teams should describe a specific, recognizable action that describes what many of the team members actually do. (Example: "What do most of us around here do at meetings? We come late, and then sit looking bored.") Give the teams 9½ minutes for this task.

4. Fold these papers into quarters. Place these in a little pile in front of each team.

5. Begin the competition. Point to one player from each team, and have them guess how many keys you have on your key chain. The team whose representative comes closest will go first.

6. Invite a player from the winning team to choose one of the folded norm sheets from the other team's pile. The player's task is to *act out* the behavioral norm described on the sheet for his or her own team. The team's task is to watch the player and guess the norm as described on the sheet as closely as possible. (*Note:* It will probably not be possible to guess word for word.) The team has 2 minutes to do this.

---

*It is far easier for people to be candid when they do not have to say, "What do *I* do?" Anyway, remember that norms are group, not individual, behaviors, and so phrasing the question this way is actually more accurate.

7. Unlike in the real game Charades, the players can talk during their presentations (except, obviously, to state what the norm is). They can also use people from the opposing team, or objects in the room, to help them depict the described norm. Each player gets up to 1 minute of planning time. The team should shout out guesses until they have Named That Norm, or until 2 minutes are up. Each time the team succeeds, it gets 10 points. Write this on the team's scoreboard.

8. After the norm has been named (or the 2-minute time limit is up), write the norm as described on a flip chart. Do not comment on the norm or invite discussion about it until the game is over.

9. Repeat the process with the second team.

10. Tally the scores on each team's scoreboard.

DEBRIEFING QUESTIONS

- It's been said that negative norms are like mushrooms—they thrive in the dark. How did it feel to hear people speak freely about the unspeakable?

- What thoughts occurred to you as you watched the negative norms being acted out? Did the behavior seem familiar? What's been the cost of this behavior in terms of your group productivity, effectiveness, team trust, and collaboration?

- How many of the norms listed were *generally recognized* by the group as problems? **KEY POINT:** This truly defines a *norm*—behavior everyone in a group recognizes as epidemic.

- *What's the one negative norm you'd most like to improve?* [Have learners vote on the norm that they feel would have the most positive impact if it were changed, and they feel most hopeful about changing. Use this norm in the next game.]

TIPS ON MAKING THIS GAME WORK WELL

Depending on the time available, you can have the teams choose more than three group norms to describe. This will increase the time spent on this game, but will also allow your group to explore more issues. (*Note:* Teams may possibly choose the same norms; this is all right, as they will likely describe the behaviors in different ways.)

Some scoring advice: 1) Be subjective when awarding points—never let the team scores get too disparate, or the losing team will start to slump perceptibly. 2) Never delete points. Instead, 3) be generous with your bonus points—they will really help to replace awkwardness with enthusiasm, ultimately inspiring your learners to communicate more openly and trustingly.

When tallying scores at the end, *definitely* repeat any contributions that got 3-point laughs! This will get a big laugh all over again (yes, even though they heard it before), and be received as a compliment by the learners who came up with the comments. All in all, it's a great way for you to *focus out* (see Chapter 1).

GROUP NORMS SHEET

Directions: With your team, choose the group norms that most affect your team's happiness, productivity, and effectiveness. Then describe how this norm is acted out in your work group in *specific, recognizable behaviors.* (Example: What do most of us around here do at meetings? We come late, and then sit looking bored.) Keep your description limited to one line.

Finish the statement: How do most people around here ...

Get (critical) feedback from others

Give (critical) feedback to others

Listen when we disagree with the speaker

Deal with customers or clients

Behave at meetings

Collaborate (help) colleagues to get a task done

Respond to conflicts

Share resources and information (data, supplies, and equipment)

GAME 3—A PERFECT WORLD

THE POINT OF THIS GAME

When making changes in our lives, it's not enough to know what we *don't* want; we have to **clearly define what we *do* want**. This game lets your learners define the positive norms they would like to see around the workplace, while helping to inspire a general attitude of positivity and hope.

TIME NEEDED

10 minutes for each norm

MATERIALS NEEDED

A flip chart or whiteboard

A SUGGESTED FUNNY INTRODUCTION

"Two construction workers, Bernie and Pete, were sitting on a girder preparing to eat lunch. Pete opened his lunch box, made a face, and said, 'Olive loaf again. I *hate* olive loaf!' Bernie thought for a minute, put down his sandwich and said, 'You know, Pete, I've been working with you for five years, and every single day you've said the same thing when you opened that box: "Olive loaf again." If you don't like olive loaf, Pete, why don't you just ask your wife to make you something different? I bet she would.' Pete looked at Bernie, surprised, and said:

"*I* make my lunches."

"If all you know is what you *don't* want, nothing will change. In the last game, we identified a negative norm—something we

204

all do that we know we don't want to do anymore. It's time to decide what we *do* want to do instead. Let's get started …."

HOW TO PLAY THIS GAME

1. Write the negative behavior from Game 2 above at the top of the flip chart or whiteboard. Then put a bold X through it.

2. Tell your learners this exercise works best when people are in a positive state of mind. Ask them to close their eyes, relax, and listen. Then read them the following:

   "We've all made the decision that we no longer want this negative norm around here. We will now imagine some really terrific behaviors to replace it. The sky is the limit. Our choices can include *any* new behaviors we think would create harmony and enjoyment at work. We are all thinking, 'If I could have *everything* the way I wanted it, what would this place be like? What would we all do differently?'

   "We realize that we spend more of our waking hours with each other than we do with our families and friends. Our jobs are a big part of our lives. What could be better than to actually *look forward* to coming to work each day, to enjoy being here, to have a workplace that we brag about to others? Other organizations have made the choice to have exactly that kind of workplace. It *can* be done. So what could we do differently here … now … every day … to accomplish the same thing for ourselves?"

3. Have your learners open their eyes. Tell them they will now compete in suggesting more positive behaviors. A person from one team will start with a suggestion. Then someone from the other team will say, "Yes, and …," and make the suggestion even better. The two teams will alternate. They will get 2 points each for 1) starting with "Yes, and" and 2) speaking in the present tense, and 3) describing *actions* rather than states of being ("We *do* this," rather than "We *are* this"). Example: One person starts out, "We return each other's calls

promptly." The person from the opposing team says: "Yes, and that's because we trust that it must be important, or the person wouldn't call." Someone from the first team adds: "Yes, and that's why we're so courteous during all internal calls." Opposing team: "Yes, and in fact we start to look *forward* to them, because we know there will be a joke, or a compliment, or some other pleasant word somewhere during the conversation." First team: "Yes, and internal calls become a big self-esteem booster, and none of us *ever* feel stress, depression, or self-doubt again!" Have them go on until they can't make the positive norm any better. Encourage them to take it to the limit by reminding them about the bonus points for creativity (and, of course, those *fabulous prizes*).

4. Toss a coin to see which team will offer the first suggestion. Write down all suggestions, no matter how far out they are. Award points (including bonus points for laughs and creativity) throughout. If at any point one team can't come up with a suggestion, toss it back to the other team.

5. When both teams have run out of suggestions, end the game. Tally up scores (again noting bonus points), and add these to the scoreboards.

DEBRIEFING QUESTIONS

- Was it hard to rephrase a negative as a positive? Did it require extra mental work?

- Why do most people go no further than to say what they *don't* want?

- How did it feel to take it all the way? Was it unrealistic to imagine a perfect world? [Answer: Probably so.] Did you come up with any ideas you might not have had if you *hadn't* taken it all the way?

- Which of the positive behaviors listed here could we put into place at work if we wanted to? Which one do you want to choose for the next game?

GAME 4—ALPHABET SOUP

THE POINT OF THIS GAME

When a group has decided to replace a negative norm with a positive one, its work is not finished. Group dynamics involve a strong element of inertia. Unless a group **makes a concerted effort to enforce a new behavior**, the group will inevitably backslide into its old ones. This  brainstorming game offers a laughter-filled way for your learners to come up with a creative plan for keeping their new, positive norm in place until it gels, or becomes second nature to everyone. (*Trainer note:* For each norm your group decides to change, it will need to come up with such an enforcement plan. Obviously, it need not play this game each time; in fact, brainstorming as a group can be done in a matter of minutes per norm.)

TIME NEEDED

20 minutes

MATERIALS NEEDED

- A flip chart
- 8½ x 11-inch paper

A SUGGESTED FUNNY INTRODUCTION

"This is a true story: One work team that decided to change its negative norms identified *backbiting* as one of its biggest annoyances. In particular, people frequently found themselves talking about Ed: Ed was sneaky, Ed was untrustworthy, Ed kissed up to the boss to avoid carrying his share of the load. The problem was ... *Ed had left the company six months before!* And everybody was *still* talking about Ed!

"They all decided they had had enough of Ed. But they also knew that group norms die hard. So they came up with a realistic way to ensure that people wouldn't fall back into 'Ed-bashing'. They set up an Ed Jar in the coffee room. After that, anyone who started complaining about Ed had to put $2 into the jar. After one week, no one ever mentioned Ed again. Thus endeth the lesson. Amen."*

[*Note:* One of your learners might ask humorously, "What did they do with the money?" Tell them soberly: "They gave it to me to carry their story to the world. Learn from it and grow, Grasshopper."]

HOW TO PLAY THIS GAME

1. Tell the group they will now brainstorm ideas for *implementing and enforcing* their new, positive norm. The only rule is that each idea offered must start with a successive letter of the alphabet. Example: If the new norm is "We return each other's calls promptly," the first idea might be, "*All* calls returned within five minutes result in a thank-you Post-It." The next might be, "*Bring* a book of riddles to work, so you can leave riddles at the end of your messages. Then other people will want to call you back to hear the answer." And so on. The teams will get 2 points for each idea and, of course, bonus points for laughs and creativity.

2. On one team's scoreboard, write out the odd-numbered letters of the Alphabet (*a, c, e, g, i,* etc.). On the other team's, write out the even-numbered letters (*b, d, f, h, j,* etc.). These will be the letters each team is responsible for.

3. Give each team several sheets of paper, and tell them they have 11½ minutes to brainstorm one idea for each letter.

---

*This story can be found in a delightful and inspiring article entitled "A Quiet Revolution," by Terry Smith, *At Work,* April 1995.

4. At the end of 11½ minutes, call time. Ask for the first idea from the A-Team (*Note:* They will *love* being called this! Apologize to the B-Team, and remind them that a rose by any other name smells as sweet. Then give them 2 points for having to endure such a brazen insult.) Write the idea on the flip chart. Note any bonus points privately on your own score sheet.

5. Now let the opposing team offer its first enforcement strategy idea. Write it down. Keep alternating between teams. If either team cannot offer an idea for one of its letters, move on to the opposing team. Carry on until the end of the alphabet is reached. Then lead everyone in a cheer for the other team.

6. Have the group vote on the enforcement strategy idea they believe will best keep them on track over the next month with their new, positive norm. (See Tips on Making This Game Work Well.) Give 10 surprise points to the team whose idea was chosen.

7. Tally the scores and add them to the team scoreboards.

DEBRIEFING QUESTIONS

- How do you feel about the way we've agreed to enforce our new, positive norm? Do you think we'll succeed?

- What else might be needed? [Answers: Often an "I remind you, you remind me" agreement between group members can be helpful. Also, scheduling a future group check-in is a powerful motivator to keep on course. Finally, many groups find that having a written agreement (see Game 5) helps to reinforce their resolve.]

- Should we focus on changing all of our norms at once? How many norms is it realistic to take on at one time?

- How many times should we get together to confront new norms? [Answer: Until you have created the workplace of your dreams! In fact, for the next few months you might want to make it a monthly practice to hold a group check-in, see how everyone has done with last month's norms, and choose the next one or two they want to work on for the following month.]

TIPS ON MAKING THIS GAME WORK WELL

If none of the ideas listed strikes your group as a winner, you can get them to go an extra step and work through an evaluation process: 1) Start with the really crazy ideas and ask, "Is there any way to save them?" If not, toss them out. 2) Categorize the remaining ideas (using any category names you like), and ask, "Are there any other ideas we could include in these categories? Any categories we've forgotten?" 3) Have the group vote on their three favorite ideas.

OTHER TOPICS THIS GAME TEACHES

- Team Building
- Creative Problem Solving

GAME 5—TAKE THE PLEDGE!

THE POINT OF THIS GAME

Once a group has decided on a course of action, its resolve to "stay the course" is often strengthened by **putting its decision in writing**. This final game in the series allows your learners to use humor in creating their own written agreement, while ending the session on a high note and giving them something to take back to the workplace with them.

TIME NEEDED

15 minutes

MATERIALS NEEDED

Paper and pens

A SUGGESTED FUNNY INTRODUCTION

"You've all done great work—give yourselves a hand! [Lead applause.]

"As you now know, workplace norms have a life of their own. We've taken a lot of thoughtful action to make sure our negative norms get out and stay out. And now for the final step: a solemn agreement that we *will* win. We won't stop until we beat those norms into the ground! There are two ways we can make our agreement: We can spit in our palms and shake hands [pause for reactions], *or* we can write it out.

"Write it out, you say? Imagine my surprise. ... Okay, let's go."

HOW TO PLAY THIS GAME

1. Give your teams 10¹⁄₃ minutes to write their agreements. Suggest they start with something momentous-sounding, like, "Be It Known to All," or "We the People." To give this last game an extra bang, tell them that this time they will get double bonus points—2, 4, and 6 points for laughs and 10 for creativity! Tell them what this means: Those numbers really add up fast, meaning either team can leap into the lead in this last activity, thus garnering those *fabulous prizes*.

2. After 10¹⁄₃ minutes, call time. Toss a coin to see which team goes first in reading its agreement aloud. Give generous bonus points. Have each team give the other team a hand.

3. Tally the final scores, and announce the winning team. And now is the moment everybody has been waiting for. Ceremoniously pull out the "fabulous prizes" ... a bag of Tootsie Roll Pops™. Hand out a pop to each member of the winning team. (Comedy tip: If it suits your personal style, you might want to make a big deal of this. Say something like, "Superlative work deserves superlative rewards. [Hand them out.] Here you are—congratulations. And here *you* are ... no please! Don't grab. I know this is exciting, but there are enough for all." Then, realizing the other team also worked hard and deserves at least some of this treasure, toss them "One to share!" Then say, "Oh, what the heck, everybody take all you want," and dump the candies out on a desk for all to grab.)

4. With their mouths full of candy, your learners can now vote on the agreement they want to use. This can be typed later using a decorative font, and sent to all at their work stations.*

5. After debriefing, finish with a commemorative photograph of the whole group. Thank everyone sincerely, and invite them to give themselves a final cheer.

*Receiving the agreement a day or two after the training session is a nice reinforcer.

DEBRIEFING QUESTIONS

- What have you learned about negativity?
- What have you learned about helplessness, the unquestioned belief that "There's nothing we can do"?
- Why do so many work groups (and individuals) choose to believe there's nothing they can do, rather than get in there and try?
- What are some of the strengths you have noticed in your fellow learners throughout this process?
- What will you personally do differently from now on when confronting negativity? What will you all do as a group?

9

Five Games to Help Employees Deal with Difficult People

GAME 1—CALM DOWN YOU BUT

THE POINT OF THIS GAME

People who successfully handle difficult interactions **avoid using trigger words whenever possible**. Sometimes the most innocuous words or phrases can really get our backs up. This is almost always because we have had past experience with such terms in loaded contexts—when these innocent-seeming words concealed negative or even hostile messages. After awhile, we can't hear these words without also hearing those negative messages. It is far easier to be aware of such words and avoid them, than to spend time conducting damage control: "That's not what I *meant*. ..."

In this game, your learners will 1) discover that they already know what many of these words are, and 2) bring the words into their everyday consciousness, thus becoming better able to stop themselves before uttering them.

TIME NEEDED

20–25 minutes

MATERIALS NEEDED

- A flip chart or whiteboard
- Lots of 8½ × 11-inch paper

A SUGGESTED FUNNY INTRODUCTION

"How many have ever told someone to [write on board] 'Calm down'? [Show of hands.] How many found that the person *didn't*? [Show of hands, laughter.] What did the person say back to you? [Your learners will almost unanimously shout, "I *am* calm!!"]

"That's right: 'I *am* calm. And if you say that again, I will *calmly* break your face.'

"Some words and phrases are like throwing gas on a fire. I call these 'fightin' words.'—They just make people come out

217

swinging. Another fightin' word is [write on board, to the right of "Calm Down"] 'You.' You made an error on this submission form; you aren't listening to what I'm telling you; you need to meet your deadlines. What's the problem with this innocent word? [Answer: It feels as if you're pointing fingers.] Right.

"Still another fightin' word is [write on board next to "You"] 'But.' I like your proposal, but we can't move on it right now; I understand your frustration, sir, but there's nothing we can do; you raise a good point, but we'll have to table it till the next meeting. What does but often mean to people? [Answer: Ignore everything I said before but.]

"We will now heighten our awareness of fightin' words, so that we can avoid throwing gas on the fire in our difficult encounters. We will do this through a game called ... [point to whiteboard and let learners read it out loud] that's right, 'Calm Down, You But.' Let's get to work!"

HOW TO PLAY THIS GAME

1. Divide learners into two teams. (Note: With larger groups, you can have up to four teams, but this means the game will take longer to play. We recommend keeping it to two teams if possible, even if they are larger than the 5 to 7 ideal size.)

2. Give the teams one minute to come up with a work-related scenario. (Examples: A customer service rep dealing with a customer or a manager giving a performance evaluation to an employee.)

3. Hand each team an 8½ × 11-inch sheet of paper, and give them 3½ minutes to brainstorm a list of fightin' words for their scenario. (Examples: "No," "That's just our policy," "I don't know," "You'll have to," "Please hold," "That's not my department," etc.) Tell them to keep their words secret—the other teams should not hear them!

4. Call time. Tell the teams they will now they have 9¼ minutes to compete in writing a one-minute script showing the best way to throw gas on a fire. Tell them that, as the judge, you will award each team:
   • 1 point for how many fightin' words they come up with;
   • 1 to 3 points for how annoying their fightin' words are;

- 5 bonus points for the actor who comes across as the most *sincere, helpful, and cooperative* when using the fightin' words! (Remind them that we often do mean to be helpful even when we're using the most annoying fightin' words. Sad, isn't it?)

5. After 9¼ minutes, call time. Give them 30 seconds to pick two actors from among themselves. While they do so, distribute a blank sheet of paper to each learner.

6. Have the first team perform their skit, while members of the other team write down whatever fightin' words they hear on their sheets of paper. At the end of the skit, have the performing team 1) identify the fightin' words they used and 2) explain, if necessary, why they're problematic. Ask the entire group to suggest alternatives to the fightin' words. Have the team member *with the neatest handwriting* note down each alternative next to its fightin' counterpart on flip chart paper.

7. Repeat the process with the second team.

8. Add up the scores. (Remember: 1 point for each fightin' word; 1, 2, or 3 points for level of *annoyance*; 5 bonus points for the most *sincere, helpful, and cooperative* actor.) *Note:* Make a point of mentioning moments in each skit that got the biggest laughs from the audience (see "Tips on Making This Game Work Well). Lead a cheer for the winning team, and award each member with a coveted Most Aggravating Communicator Award (see handout).

9. Make copies of the lists of fightin' words and their alternatives, and distribute to each learner. Encourage them to post the lists in their workplace for the next few weeks.

DEBRIEFING QUESTIONS

[*Note:* Much debriefing has already taken place in the form of learners explaining their lists and suggesting alternatives. While you don't want to flog this subject to death, here are some questions you can ask if they seem pertinent to the occasion.]

- Many of us agreed on what constituted fightin' words—that is, we felt we'd be irritated if someone said them to us. Yet how many would admit to having used these same words to others? Why do we sometimes use words or phrases to others that would get our own backs up?

- Did anyone hear any words or phrases you *didn't* know were fighting words? (In other words, that wouldn't bother *you* if someone said them to you?) How does that happen?

- If you make an innocent comment that someone else hears as fightin' words, does that make you a jerk? Does it make them wrong? Which would you say is more important: your intentions or the other person's interpretation of your statement?

- What's probably the best thing to do if we inadvertently say something that is perceived as fightin' words? [Answer: Apologize sincerely and move on.]

TIPS ON MAKING THIS GAME WORK WELL

When telling teams their scores, don't itemize publicly! Otherwise, you'll lose precious time as your learners will nickel-and-dime you to death—trust us on this one. Just say something like, "For *the total number* of fightin' words, X Team gets a total of __ points. For *how annoying* their Fightin' Words were, __ points. [*Tip:* Definitely repeat any 3-pointers! This will get a howl of laughter, and the learners who came up with them will glow.] And *now* ... the actor who came across as the most irritatingly *sincere, helpful, and cooperative* was. ... _____! Congratulations! Five bonus points for your team!" [*Note:* Usually all your learners will agree on who was most irritating, and everyone will love this moment.]

OTHER TOPICS THIS GAME TEACHES

- Communication Skills
- Management Skills
- Speaking Skills
- Emotional Intelligence
- Reducing Workplace Negativity
- Customer Service
- Conflict and Negotiation

Certificate

May it be known

BY ALL

WHO READ THIS THAT

THIS CERTIFICATE HAS BEEN PRESENTED TO

_____

FOR

MOST AGGRAVATING COMMUNICATOR

OFFICIAL SEAL

_____
ORGANIZATION

PRESENTED THIS _____ DAY OF _____, 20 _____

_____
SIGNED

221

GAME 2—MIRROR, MIRROR

THE POINT OF THIS GAME

People who successfully handle difficult interactions tend to **modify their communication style to make others more comfortable**. If their communication partners are a little quieter than they are, for example, they might bring down their own speaking volume. If their partners make lots of eye  contact, they follow suit. If the partners keep to business topics and avoid personal subjects, they will do the same, and so on. Psychologists alternately term this behavior blending, pacing, mirroring, and synchrony. (We refer to it as synchrony in this game.) Professional communicators of all kinds make a point of mastering this easy skill, because it is shown to *reduce emotional distance* between people.

In this game, your learners get to witness the power of synchrony.

TIME NEEDED

15–20 minutes

MATERIALS NEEDED

- A 3 × 5-inch card or sheet of 8½ × 11-inch paper for half of your learners
- *Person B (Left and Right)* handouts for half of your learners

PREPARATION

For maximum impact, play and debrief this game before you explain the concept of synchrony. This game illustrates the synchrony phenomenon, along with its opposite, dyssemia (using communication styles that are *different* from those of one's

222

partner). Having played this game, your learners should be more interested in and receptive to using synchrony techniques.*

A SUGGESTED FUNNY INTRODUCTION

[*Note:* This is not roaringly hilarious, but it does inspire amused curiosity.]

"How many have ever noticed that you can watch two people from across a crowded room and tell whether or not they're getting along? Whether they're in *accord* with each other? [Show of hands. *Note:* Virtually every hand will go up.]

"Interesting. So we're all psychic.

"Okay, how many want to show off your psychic powers?

"I knew you would. (I'm psychic, too.) So ... everybody up!"

HOW TO PLAY THIS GAME

1. Divide learners into pairs by simply asking them to pair up with the person sitting next to them.

2. Mentally (not out loud) divide the room in half, by whatever means most expedient for you. (*Hint:* If there is an aisle down the middle of the room, with learners seated on either side, your work is done for you.) *Your pairs will now be either Left-siders or Right-siders to you.*

3. Have the pairs establish which of them has the most credit cards in his or her wallet. (*Note:* They only have to *tell,* not *show.*) That will be Person A. The other will be Person B. Have Persons B raise their hands.

4. Pass out the handouts to the hand-raisers, taking care to give the left-sider Persons B the handouts marked *LEFT,* and the right-sider Persons B the handouts marked. ... (Oh, let's see if you can guess.) Unbeknownst to your learners, the handouts will have two different sets of instructions. In one set, Persons B will mirror their partners' nonverbal behavior. In

*For quick explanations of both synchrony and dyssemia, see Chapter 8 of *Emotional Intelligence,* Daniel Goleman (Bantam Books, New York, 1995).

the other set, Persons B are asked to do the opposite of their partners' behavior.

5. Ask the Persons B to study their handouts silently. In the meantime, pass out a card or paper to Persons A, and ask them to write down two or three of their work-related pet hates, or types of people that annoy them. These can include whiny customers, intrusive sales reps, people who don't return my calls, or anything else they come up with.

6. Now tell Persons A they have 3 minutes to describe their pet hates to Persons B. Tell them that as they do so, their partners will respond only with head nods, or maybe the occasional "Mm-hm" or "I see." It will be Persons A's job to use their psychic powers to tell *whether their partner is in accord with them or not.*

7. After 3 minutes, call time and ask your learners to shake hands, say, "Nice complaining with you," and face front.

DEBRIEFING QUESTIONS

- How many A's felt you and your partner were on the same page? [Show of hands.]

  (Note: *It is extremely likely that more of the Persons A on the left side of the room will raise their hands than on the right side. This is probably because their partners used synchrony. Point this out when it happens; the visual confirmation is very powerful! In cases when it doesn't happen, you might want to investigate further. Often you will find that the Persons B in question didn't mirror very much or at all. Of course, there could be other reasons, and that's useful information too. You could ask the As what tipped them off one way or another.*)

- [Now have one Person B from each side of the room read the instructions on the handout aloud. This is a good time to explain synchrony (or, as your Persons B now call it, mirroring) and dyssemia.]

- How many are aware that you tend to mirror people you like or agree with, and you do this *every day*? How many knew you do the opposite with people you *don't* like or agree with?

- Why do so many professional communicators practice mirroring even people they don't like? [Answer: Their livelihoods depend on *connecting with others*.]
- How many Persons B felt self-conscious while mirroring your partners? Why?
- Is mirroring manipulative? [*Note*: Some of your learners will cry, "Yes!"] If so, is it also manipulative to wear different clothes to church from those you would wear to a party? Or to speak to your boss differently from the way you speak to your sister? [Answer: Actually, yes. So welcome to socialized behavior! We are manipulative *whenever* we modify our behavior to suit the occasion.]
- **KEY POINT:** So is it necessarily *bad* to be manipulative?
- Homework: Over the next week, start noticing the mirroring that goes on all around you. In the following week, start mirroring at least one thing in every conversation you have. Some people do it instinctively, and studies show they tend to be trusted more than people who don't. If this behavior is not instinctive for you, learn it! And remember, Grasshopper, use it only for good.

OTHER TOPICS THIS GAME TEACHES

- Assertiveness
- Communication Skills
- Leadership Skills
- Management Skills
- Facilitation Skills
- Speaking Skills
- Conflict and Negotiation
- Customer Service

PERSON B (LEFT)

As your partner describes a pet peeve to you, do not verbally agree or disagree! You may nod to show you heard, or say things like, "Mm-hm," or "I see," but that's it.

Your main job is to **observe your partner's nonverbal behaviors, and mirror any of the more common ones**. These can include: head tilting or nodding, leaning forward (or back), facial expression, making little (or lots of) eye contact, crossing arms (or legs or ankles), putting hands in pockets, etc.

Two tips:

1. Don't mirror your partner immediately. Let half a minute or so pass before you get into synch with him or her.

2. Don't do *exactly* as your partner does, but do something similar. For instance, if he crosses his arms, you can fold yours; if she puts her hands in her pockets, you can put yours in your belt loops or on your hips, etc.

As your partner describes a pet peeve to you, do not verbally agree or disagree! You may nod to show you heard, or say things like, "Mm-hm," or "I see," but that's it.

Your main job is to **observe your partner's nonverbal behaviors and do the opposite**. For instance, if he tilts or nods his head, you keep yours centered or still. If she leans forward, you lean back. Have a slightly different facial expression from his. If she makes lots of eye contact, you make only a little. If he crosses his arms (or legs or ankles), you don't, and so on.

Tip: Don't make your moves immediately. Let half a minute or so pass before you do the opposite of whatever your partner is doing.

GAME 3—NAME THAT QUADRANT!

THE POINT OF THIS GAME

People who successfully handle difficult interactions can **identify and respond to different behavior types**. This game gives your learners practice in recognizing a variety of behaviors and "reading" the needs underlying them.

TIME NEEDED

10–15 minutes

MATERIALS NEEDED

Behavior matrix (see handout), reproduced on overhead or flip chart

PREPARATION

This game should be played after introducing your learners to the well-known concept of behavioral types using the crossed-spectra matrix presented at the end of this game.

In the matrix, the vertical spectrum represents a person's interest or *focus*. People who are above the center mark tend to be more interested in tasks—objects, ideas, numbers, and so on. These people would likely pick professions like engineering, accounting, or computer programming. Those who are below the center tend to be more interested in people—emotions, relationships, and so on. Such people lean more toward professions like teaching, psychology, sales, or ministry.

The horizontal spectrum represents a person's *style of communicating*. People to the left of center are more introverted, while people to the right of center are more extroverted. Going clockwise from the upper left, the four quadrants show 1) more introverted individuals who are more focused on tasks (Scientists); 2) more extroverted individuals who are also more focused on tasks (Directors); 3) individuals who are more extroverted and more focused on people (Entertainers); 4) individuals who are more introverted and also more focused on people (Nurturers).

In a huge oversimplification, the Scientist values *technical accuracy*—every *i* dotted, every *t* crossed. The Director, on the other hand, is happiest with *quick completion* ("Let's move—we've got a deadline"). *Receiving attention* is a major motivator for the Entertainer, while the Nurturer is most comfortable when there is *harmony among people.**

A SUGGESTED FUNNY INTRODUCTION

"Okay, everyone, now that you're clear on the concept of behavior types and their needs, it's time to play *Name That Quadrant!*"

"Yes, folks, it's the game in which you observe people's verbal and nonverbal behavior, and try to guess whether they value details, deadlines, drama, or devotion to others. And now let's *get going!*"

[*Note:* Bonus points for a really good impersonation of an annoying game-show host. Also, consider having your learners stand up for this quick activity, if only to provide variety and a physical break from sitting.]

HOW TO PLAY THIS GAME

1. As the game show host, ask learners to match the following depictions to the four behavior types.

2. Describe four kinds of clothing, one after the other, and then have learners match them to their probable quadrant:

*For a more detailed explanation of the matrix, and another example of a matrix, see Drs. Rick Brinkman and Rick Kirschner, *Dealing with People You Can't Stand* (New York: McGraw-Hill, 1994).

a. An expensive but conservative navy pinstripe suit. (Director)

b. An Armani "power suit" with $70 hand-painted silk tie or scarf. (Entertainer)

c. "Friends of the Library" outfit: mid-calf length dirndl skirt, flat pumps, soft Norwegian-knit sweater over white blouse with Peter-Pan collar. (Nurturer)

d. Rumpled corduroy slacks, sneakers, mismatched socks, and a pocket-protector. (Scientist)

3. Name these four cars and have your learners assign one to each quadrant:

a. A red sportscar. (Entertainer)

b. A prestigious silver sedan. (Director)

c. A white minivan with bumper stickers that read, "Commit random acts of kindness" and "Have you hugged your kid today?" (Nurturer)

d. A car with the best mileage and highest EPA rating and resale value according to this month's *Consumer Reports* magazine. (Scientist)

4. Have four of your learners ask you what time it is.

a. Tap your watch and say, "Um, well, my watch says 11:17, but that might not be exact, it seems to lose 13 seconds per week, which shouldn't happen because the computer chip is okay or else the watch calculator wouldn't work, so maybe the electromagnetic spectrum is being affected by sunspot activity. ..." (Scientist)

b. "Oh, dear, is that lovely watch of yours broken? Here, take mine." (Nurturer)

c. "Time for a *brew*! Ha, ha!" (Entertainer)

d. "It's ten o'clock." (Director)

5. Ask four of your learners to say, "Wanna to go to lunch?" to you.

a. "Oh, thank you so much for asking. Is now a good time for you? Want me to drive? You look tired." (Nurturer)

b. "Okay. Meet you at the car. Five minutes." (Director)

c. "Um, I don't know. When did you want to leave? Where are we going? How far is it? What's on the menu? I can't take anything acidic. Is Harry going to be there? I don't like Harry. ..." (Scientist)

d. *"Love* to! Say, listen, I know a *fabulous* spot. I take *everyone* there. The staff *loves* me—always gives me the *best* table. ..." (Entertainer)

6. Congratulate your learners on their excellent analytical skills, and invite them to sit down.

DEBRIEFING QUESTIONS

- Remind your learners that in this game you played *stereotypes*—you exaggerated behaviors like crazy! Nonetheless, do people's choices of clothes, cars, words, topics, and so on reveal something about their deeper values?

- What gifts or added perspectives does each behavioral type offer? How does each help your group move forward?

- Think of people you prefer being with. Typically, which behavioral quadrant do they fall into? What does this suggest about your preferred style?

- Do people always stay in the same quadrant? [Answer: No. Most people have a preferred behavior, and another with which they are secondarily comfortable. Example: Entertainers may adopt Director behavior when a deadline forces them to be more task-focused. A minority of people seem equally comfortable operating in any quadrant the occasion demands. And no matter which quadrant you normally operate in, when tax time rolls around, you'd better high-tail it into the Scientist quadrant so you can fill those forms out correctly and completely!]

- What other behaviors have you seen people (or yourself) exhibit that suggest they're in a specific quadrant *at that moment*?

- Can we ever say, "I know what quadrant you're in, so I know what you'll do in any situation"? **KEY POINT:** We should never use behavior-type indicators to pigeonhole people. It's like spitting into the wind.

TIPS ON MAKING THIS GAME WORK WELL

When delivering your response lines, try to get as completely into character as possible. For instance, the two less *assertive* types (Scientist and Nurturer, left side of the horizontal spectrum) will tend to speak relatively softly—maybe even a bit hesitantly in the case of the Nurturer, or indecisively in the case of the Scientist. These two types may also be more physically pulled in, for example, less given to expansive hand gestures. Another example: The two more *task-oriented* types (Scientist and Director, top end of the vertical spectrum) might tend toward less vocal modulation, eye contact, and other kinds of personal contact. In the case of the Scientist, this might be shyness. In the case of Directors, they may be visually scouting the room to make sure everyone is doing their work.

Remember, you are *exaggerating* these types' qualities, and that's okay for the purpose of this learning game. Just be sure to acknowledge the fact during the debriefing.

OTHER TOPICS THIS GAME TEACHES

- Leadership Skills
- Management Skills
- Conflict and Negotiation
- Dealing with Stress
- Customer Service

BEHAVIOR-TYPE MATRIX

Task

SCIENTIST   DIRECTOR

Introverted   Extroverted

NURTURER   ENTERTAINER

People

GAME 4—PICKIN' UP THOSE VIBES

THE POINT OF THIS GAME

People who successfully handle difficult interactions **are aware of how their feelings and attitudes affect their nonverbal message**. They know their listeners will "hear" their tone of voice, vocal volume, rate of speech, and body language *over and above their words*. This game will let your learners experience how loudly these nonverbal components of communication can "speak."

TIME NEEDED

25 minutes

MATERIALS NEEDED

- One copy of the Attitude Sheet for Person 2(A) (see handout)
- One copy of the Attitude Sheet for Person 2(B) (see handout)
- Three copies of the Role-Play Script (see handout)
- One Observation Sheet (see handout) for each learner who watches the role-play

A SUGGESTED FUNNY INTRODUCTION

"Who's comfortable doing a role-play in front of others?"

[*Note:* Occasionally you'll get one or two volunteers immediately, but usually not a single hand will go up. This is okay; experience has shown us there are Entertainers in every crowd,

234

and some of them secretly love to do role-plays. Have faith! Keep going:]

"Who would be willing to demonstrate this learning point for me? To make this clear for your fellow-learners? To help me out ... to *really* help me out here ... to *really* do me a *big* favor?" [Play up the role of a person who asks brightly, trying not to look like he or she is really begging. For some reason, this always gets volunteers.] "Thank you! I need three volunteers."

HOW TO PLAY THIS GAME

1. Hand a copy of the script to each of your three volunteers. Tell two of the volunteers that they will play Persons 2 (A and B) and give them their attitude sheets. Ask all the volunteers to go offstage until called.

2. Hand out the Observation Sheets to the rest of the learners. Instruct them that their job is to watch for nonverbal cues that will let them answer the questions on their sheets.

3. Give everyone a moment to look over their printed materials.

4. Call Person 1 and Person 2 (A) to the front and have them do the role-play.

5. Have the learners complete their Observation Sheets for Scene 1.

6. Repeat the role-play with Person 2(B) and again have the learners complete their Observation Sheets.

7. Lead applause for the three actors, and begin debriefing.

DEBRIEFING QUESTIONS

Start by working from the Observation Sheet. After the learners have shared their impressions of the situation based on the nonverbal cues they observed, ask:

- So, did the exchange go differently from one time to the next?
- If so, *why* do you think the same conversation went differently at two different times?

- To Person 1: How did you feel when talking with the first Person 2? The second?

  Now have the two Persons 2 stand and read their Attitude Sheets aloud.

- Has anybody ever had the experience of trying to be courteous to someone you didn't like, and found the person kept on responding negatively to you? Do you think the person picked up on your nonverbal message over and above your verbal one? [*Joke:* Was anybody's nonverbal message, "I hate you"?]

- How can we get better control of our nonverbal communication, *especially* when our underlying thought is negative? [Possible answers: Find a way to blow off steam before trying to engage this person in a fruitful conversation; when all else fails, we can use mirroring (see Game 2) to reduce emotional distance.]

TIPS ON MAKING THIS GAME WORK WELL

The reason the attitudes are written on full sheets paper instead of on small slips is to give your observers the impressions that Persons 2 have complex sets of instructions to carry out. The idea is to make the point that the nonverbal message underlying the verbal one can often be very simple (not to mention *having nothing to do with what's being said*).

OTHER TOPICS THIS GAME TEACHES

- Emotional Intelligence
- Assertiveness
- Communication Skills
- Customer Service

ATTITUDE SHEET: PERSON 2 (A)

You have a strong feeling toward your role-play partner. As you work from the script, keep this thought in the forefront of your mind at all times:

"I REALLY LIKE YOU."

You don't have to do anything special—just keep thinking this thought.

ATTITUDE SHEET: PERSON 2(B)

You have a strong feeling toward your role-play partner. As you work from the script, keep this thought in the forefront of your mind at all times:

"I REALLY HATE YOU."

Please don't do anything special—just keep thinking this thought.

ROLE-PLAY SCRIPT

HANDOUT

PERSON 1: Hi, _____, How are you doing?

PERSON 2: Oh, hi. Fine, _____, how are you?

PERSON 1: Just fine. _____, do you have a minute?

PERSON 2: Sure.

PERSON 1: You know the pitch we're doing for Hershey's next week?

PERSON 2: Uh-huh.

PERSON 1: Well, I'd like you to handle our slides, if you can.

PERSON 2: Um … sure, I can do that. I'm sure I can fit it in....

PERSON 1: Oh, that would be great. You always do such a good job on the vi-suals. Now, they need to be ready for Monday. Is that a problem?

PERSON 2: Nooo. …

PERSON 1: That's not very much lead time, I know. Have you got many other commitments just now? I don't want to stack your plate too high.

PERSON 2: Well, I do have quite a lot in my "In" basket. …

PERSON 1: What's the priority on the other projects?

PERSON 2: Well, there's only one that's *really* urgent, I guess.

PERSON 1: That's not too bad. When is it due?

PERSON 2: This Friday.

PERSON 1: How long do you think it will take?

PERSON 2: Definitely the rest of today. Probably half of tomorrow. Maybe *all* of tomorrow. It's hard to say. …

PERSON 1: Okay, how about this: If you made a phone call to Creative *now*, they could start finding images while you work on your project. By the time you're finished tomorrow, they should have what you need.

PERSON 2: That should work.

PERSON 1: If you run into anything unexpected, don't hesitate to give me a call. I can always roll up my sleeves and help out. That's what team-mates are for. Together we can get this done. Thanks a lot, _____.

PERSON 2: No problem.

OBSERVATION SHEET

1. Was Person 2 interested in doing the job Person 1 asked?

    First scene: Yes____   No____

    Why? _____

    Second scene: Yes____   No____

    Why? _____

2. Was Person 2 confident in his or her ability?

    First scene: Yes____   No____

    Why? _____

    Second scene: Yes____   No____

    Why? _____

3. Did Person 2 understand or agree with the suggestions Person 1 made?

    First scene: Yes____   No____

    Why? _____

    Second scene: Yes____   No____

    Why? _____

4. Was Person 2 resentful of being asked to do this?

    First scene: Yes____   No____

    Why? _____

    Second scene: Yes____   No____

    Why? _____

GAME 5—SCRIPTS

THE POINT OF THIS GAME

People who successfully handle difficult interactions often **prepare in advance for encounters they expect to be difficult**. Besides talking to trusted friends or colleagues, reading self-help books, or taking communication training, they may plan specific strategies—

sometimes even writing scripts—for dealing with difficult people in ways they think will be most effective.

TIME NEEDED

45 minutes to an hour

MATERIALS NEEDED

- Bully, Ninja, and Whiner Scripts (see handouts)
- Bully, Ninja, and Whiner Observation Sheets (see handouts)

A SUGGESTED FUNNY INTRODUCTION

"How many have ever run into a *Bully*—you know, the person who makes things happen through intimidation? [Imitate:] 'What do you think you're doing? *Correlating*? Are you nuts? That report is due tomorrow! You've been at it for a week, and you're already two weeks behind! Okay, I'm going to tell you your next three moves. Stop working and prepare to take notes. ...' [Show of hands, snickers.]

"How many have ever known a *Ninja*—someone who doesn't come right out and tell you anything's wrong, but just bides some time, and at exactly the right moment takes a well-aimed potshot right at your liver? [Imitate, whispering to someone else behind your hand:] 'Well, *that's* an interesting comment—if you're brain-dead.' If you ask, 'What did you say?' what do they always answer? [Learners will gleefully fill in: 'Nothing!']

"What about the *Whiner*—ever met one of those? [Imitate:] '*Everything* is wrong, and I can't do *anything* about it because *nobody* listens to me, that's the way it was at my *last* job, and isn't that *always* the way, so don't ask me to do *anything* because I *can't*!' Anyone ever meet a Whiner? [Show of hands, lots of venting laughter.]

"These are the three most common difficult people—they're everywhere! All of us will face Bullies, Ninjas, and Whiners again and again throughout our personal and professional lives. That's the bad news. The good news is that, since we know these difficult people are coming, we can prepare for them.

"Can we make this fun—or at least less stressful? I think so! Let's learn how to do that. …"

HOW TO PLAY THIS GAME

1. Ask for six volunteers. (*Note:* If no one volunteers, pick eight people who *secretly* want to. How will you know who they are? Easy; the ones who really *don't* want to take part will suddenly become intensely interested in their workbooks! In other words, anyone who makes eye contact with you for at least two seconds is practically a sure bet. Trust us on this one: Just look at a "volunteer" for two seconds, then say, "Will *you?*" Almost always, they will duck their heads, feign unwillingness, and say, "Sure, okay." This is a very human moment. Enjoy it.)

2. Divide the volunteers into pairs, and give each pair two copies of either the Bully, Ninja, or Whiner scripts. Then hand out copies of all three Observations Sheets to the rest of your learners. Allow everyone one or two minutes to look over their printed materials.

3. Ask the pair with the Bully script to come to the front and perform the Bully role-play. When they finish, have the observers fill out their Observation Sheets.

4. Repeat the process for the Ninja and Whiner role-plays. Have everyone not involved in each role-play fill out an Observation Sheet.

5. Lead applause for the actors, and debrief using the Observation Sheets.

6. Have your learners break up into pairs. Partners now describe to each other an experience they have had with one of these difficult types. By turns, one partner acts out the person described, and the other tries out the behaviors outlined on the Observation Sheet.

7. Have them shake hands, say, "Boy, you were a real pain in the neck—thanks!" and resume their seats.

DEBRIEFING QUESTIONS

- How did it feel to try out these new strategies?
- Is it hard to change our own behavior, even when we have good reason to think it will change the difficult person's behavior?
- How many would say your old way of dealing with difficult people hasn't worked for you very well?
- What are some obstacles you see in putting these new strategies into place in your own life?

TIPS ON MAKING THIS GAME WORK WELL

An alternate use for this game is to introduce and review behavioral objectives and strategies for dealing with difficult people. Start out by role-playing from the scripts, with you in the role of the person responding to the difficult person. Have your learners fill out their Observation Sheets, trying to identify the strategies you used. Then conduct your training, naming and discussing these strategies. At the end of the module, repeat the role-plays, allowing your learners to again fill out their Observation Sheets. This time, they should be able to define the strategies more accurately.

OTHER TOPICS THIS GAME TEACHES

- Assertiveness
- Communication Skills
- Conflict and Negotiation
- Customer Service

SCRIPTS

SCRIPT: THE BULLY

You and your colleagues are in a meeting with your team. Person 2 has been delivering a report to the group. Suddenly, Person 1 explodes. (Person 2: Use Person 1's name for this role-play.)

PERSON 1: Hey, *hey, hey!* This has gone on long enough!

PERSON 2: *(Maintain eye contact and let person 1 vent for a moment.)*

PERSON 1: You're wasting *my* time, and the time of *every person here.* Did you even *prepare* for this meeting? This long-winded "report" of yours just goes on and on—and *then* you can't even answer Rodney's simple *question.*

PERSON 2: Barbara. Barbara. *(Or whatever your partner's name is. Keep your tone of voice respectful and calm. Maintain eye contact. Remember to breathe!)*

PERSON 1: This is ridiculous. I say we stop this farce right now, and give the project to someone who knows what the heck they're doing! Then we might get some *intelligent* information at next week's meeting.

PERSON 2: *(More forcefully:)* Barbara.

PERSON 1 I've got better things to do. I'm outta here. ...

PERSON 2: *(Decisively:)* Barbara. I need to interrupt you here. I see that you think my report is long-winded. But I hope you'll feel differently in just a moment. Now, I'm going to finish my presentation, and when I do, I'll be happy to address any questions you have.

(Turn immediately to everyone else:) Now, as I was saying. ...

245

SCRIPT: THE NINJA

You are in a meeting to share ideas about developing a new market for your company's product. Person 1 has an idea and is trying to share it with the group: consultation services specifically aimed at electronics firms that are having problems getting and keeping good employees. Person 2 keeps taking potshots at it.

PERSON 1:   ... So with the retention problem so widespread in the software industry, I think we've found ourselves a real niche—

PERSON 2:   *(To the person next to you)* Yeah, and the "niche" is in her head.

PERSON 1:   Pardon me? Did you say something?

PERSON 2:   *(Innocently)* No.

PERSON 1:   Okay. Now, it's important to note that if we move on this, we'll be the first ones in the market—

PERSON 2:   *(To the person next to you)* Do the words "where angels fear to tread" mean anything to you?

PERSON 1:   Sorry, is there something you wanted to add?

PERSON 2:   No, no!

PERSON 1:   You're sure?

PERSON 2:   Yes.

PERSON 1:   Okie-dokie. Now, as I was saying—

PERSON 2:   *(To other person)* I can't believe this.

PERSON 1:   Pardon me?

PERSON 2:   Nothing! Let's move on.

PERSON 1:   It's obvious you do have either a question or an opinion to express. I'm happy to hear it.

PERSON 2: All right, if you insist. I think there's no *way* this flaky idea of yours is going to work. Our services aren't *appropriate* to the electronics industry, for gosh sake!

PERSON 1: What makes you think so?

PERSON 2: Because scientists run it! They'll never buy a service to help them humanize their workplace. They don't *care* about that—they're barely human themselves! Outreaching to them is a waste of marketing money, and that money is sorely needed for other projects—or don't you read your e-mail?

PERSON 1: So you don't think this merits even a preliminary feasibility study?

PERSON 2: I think that's what I just said. *Duh*!

PERSON 1: Okay, so you think I'm trying to sell hamburgers to vegetarians. (Look around at other participants.) What does everyone else think?

PERSON 1:   Hey, _____. Will those files be ready for the client meeting tomorrow?

PERSON 2:   *(In a nasally voice:)* I *know* I'm supposed to have them ready, but my in-basket is so *full,* and I can't get a temp because of the budget cutbacks, and *anyway* I think I'm coming down with a *cold,* but I can't take the time *off* because you can lose your *job* for being sick at this place, which is totally *illegal,* and it's probably *allergies* because of the *ventilation* system, which I've talked to *Maintenance* about, as well as my *chair* which cuts into my *back,* but *they* don't care. . . .

PERSON 1:   Hmm. So you're overloaded *and* you're feeling under the weather. Sounds like you're having a tough time today. Okay, what would help?

PERSON 2:   I *told* you! Nothing can be done because I can't have a temp!

PERSON 1:   Well, you know best! Okay, so if you don't get help, what are some other options? We have to have those files for the meeting tomorrow. That's *not* an option.

PERSON 2:   Well, I'll just tell everyone else that wants me to do something for them that they can just do it themselves.

PERSON 1:   I imagine you *could,* [laughing] although then you'd be having the same conversation with them as you are now with me. I know it's rough. In the meantime, what can you do to help me out? These files are urgent.

PERSON 2:   They're *all* urgent! Everything is due yesterday around here!

PERSON 1:   Well, sometimes it seems that way, that's for sure.

PERSON 2:   Yeah, and it all falls on *my* shoulders!

PERSON 1: I know the feeling. When can I get these files from you?

PERSON 2: Well, I guess around 10 o'clock.

PERSON 1: Great! I'll write that down in my appointment book. I'll be by to pick them up at ten. Thanks, _____ I appreciate you're help on this.

PERSON 2: *(In a resentful whine:)* You're *welcome.*

OBSERVATION SHEET—THE BULLY

The steps to use with these difficult people are:

1. **Hold your ground.** How did you see this happen?

   _____

   _____

   _____

2. **Interrupt their interruption.** How did you see this happen?

   _____

   _____

   _____

3. **Acknowledge their concerns.** How did you see this happen?

   _____

   _____

   _____

4. **Reclaim control.** How did you see this happen?

   _____

   _____

   _____

OBSERVATION SHEET—THE NINJA

The steps to use with these difficult people are:

1. **Stop and respond to *every* sniping comment immediately.** (If they can't hide, they can't snipe.) How did you see this happen?

   _____

   _____

   _____

2. **Ask questions instead of arguing.** How did you see this happen?

   _____

   _____

   _____

3. **Restate their concerns *respectfully*.** How did you see this happen?

   _____

   _____

   _____

4. **Check your own perceptions.** (No matter how annoying ninjas are, they *may* have a point!) How did you see this happen?

   _____

   _____

   _____

OBSERVATION SHEET—THE WHINER

The steps to use with these difficult people are:

1. Let them vent a little first. How did you see this happen?

_____

_____

2. Separate the wheat from the chaff, and restate their *main* problem(s). How did you see this happen?

_____

_____

3. Acknowledge their emotions. How did you see this happen?

_____

_____

4. *Don't solve their problems!* (Ask them to come up with solutions. *But expect them to refuse*—at least for now.) How did you see this happen?

_____

_____

5. Try gentle humor for the really outrageous complaints. How did you see this happen?

_____

_____

6. Get the whiner to commit to an action. (End the exchange after this commitment is reached.) How did you see this happen?

_____

_____

10

Five Games to Take the Fear Out of Assertiveness

GAME 1—SCULPTURES

THE POINT OF THIS GAME

Assertive people are **consistent in their verbal and nonverbal communication**. This game helps your learners identify and deliver consistent assertive messages.

TIME NEEDED

20 minutes

MATERIALS NEEDED

A flip chart, overhead, or whiteboard

PREPARATION

Your learners need to be familiar with the verbal and nonverbal characteristics of assertiveness, as well as the concept of congruent and incongruent messages, before beginning this game.

A SUGGESTED FUNNY INTRODUCTION

"How many have ever heard the saying, 'Fake it till you make it'? [Show of hands; usually you'll get one or two knowing chuckles.] "What this means, of course, is that if you want to become good at a new skill, often the shortest route is to act as if you already *are*. This idea is not new. A couple of thousand years ago, Plato was asked, 'How does a man become brave?' He answered, 'By doing brave things.' (Back then people only talked about men; wasn't that a quaint idea?) So ... how many would like to become braver? [Show of hands.] Okay, let's go!"

HOW TO PLAY THIS GAME

1. Ask the group to brainstorm three situations in which they would find it hard to act assertively. List these on a flip chart, overhead, or whiteboard.

2. Now get six volunteers. If no one volunteers, pick six people who *secretly* want to. (*Note:* How will you know who they are? Easy; the ones who really *don't* want to take part will suddenly become intensely interested in their workbooks! In other words, anyone who makes eye contact with you for at least two seconds is practically a sure bet. Trust us on this one. Just look at a "volunteer" and say, "Will *you?*" They will almost always duck their heads, feign unwillingness, and say, "Well, okay." This is a very human moment. Enjoy it.)

3. Have your volunteers join you at the front of the room, three standing on your left and three on your right.

4. Now go into character as a French Master Sculptor. Turn to the three volunteers on your left and say: "Welcome to my world-famous institute, *L'Ecole des Snooty Artistes.* It is natural that you would come to learn at my feet, since I am the greatest sculptor the world has ever known. My works are so lifelike, so full of *la vie,* that they actually talk! *Oui!* They talk. No one knows how I do this, and of course you, my disciples, will never tell. But today you will learn my secret. And then you, too, will be able to amaze the ignorant art-buying public and empty their fat wallets for them. *Vive la France! Vive les Snooty Artistes!*" (Note: Bonus points for putting on a bad French accent. And if your learners groan—which they should if they have any taste—just remember Chapter 1, and take a bow: "Thank you. Thank you very much!")

5. Now choose one of the difficult situations the group brainstormed. Ask the group to brainstorm a list of assertive statements someone could make in that situation. Write these on flip chart paper.

6. Pair up the "art students" on your left with the three people on your right. The three people on your right are the "sculptures" that the artists will pose by arranging their arms, legs, and even facial features to relate to the difficult situation you chose.

7. Assign each pair an attitude to portray. One of the "sculptures" must be made to look assertive, one aggressive, and one passive. For example, if the situation is, say, an employee being chewed out by the boss, the assertive "sculpture" might show someone listening with a respectful expression and open body posture, the passive one might cringe, and the aggressive one might stand with hands on hips and a defiant look. (Tip: Be on guard for the one-fingered salute!) When the "art students" have finished, have them say, "Voila!" and stand back.

8. While the artists are arranging their hands, feet, and faces, the "sculptures" should mentally choose one of the assertive responses that were brainstormed by the group. When the artists are finished the "sculptures" will be asked to say this statement out loud.

9. Introduce each artist one by one and ask them to "explain" their sculpture and how it depicts the assigned attitude and situation. Ask the artist to press a "button" on the sculpture. That is the sculpture's cue to say the chosen statement while remaining in the pose.

10. After all three have spoken, say "*Bravo!*" Lead applause for *les artistes*, and allow the sculptures to relax.

11. Shuffle the three sculptures so that each one is now assigned a new aggressive, passive, or assertive attitude.

12. Ask the group to brainstorm responses to the second difficult situation and write these on the flip chart paper. Repeat the same process as in round one.

13. Do it one last time with the third difficult situation. By now, each of the three sculptures will have had the experience of making an assertive statement in an assertive, a passive,

and an aggressive pose. Thank all your artistic geniuses, perhaps finishing with one last, rousing, *"Vive les Snooty Artistes!"*

DEBRIEFING QUESTIONS

- What did the assertive sculptures have in common in terms of the way they looked? If you saw a person in this pose in real life, what would you assume about the person?

  To the sculptures:

- How did it feel when your pose matched your words?
- How about when it didn't? Did it feel convincing to you?
- How did it feel to be molded? Did your pose feel natural to your personality?
- Was there an assertive statement you had to make that you might not make in real life? Did your assertive pose help you to fake it?
- Did your physical postures influence the way you spoke— tone of voice, rate of speed, or volume?

  To the class:

- What did you observe when a sculpture's body language matched his or her verbal language?
- How about when it didn't? How convincing was the assertive statement coming from a nonassertive posture?
- What would happen if these sculptures came to life and were real people in these situations? Would they have convinced you? How would you know if they were faking it?
- **KEY POINT:** When we talk in real life with someone whose verbal and nonverbal messages are *not consistent,* which message do we usually believe?

TIPS ON MAKING THIS GAME WORK WELL

If you have more time, it's an excellent idea to divide the class into pairs and have them practice making one of the assertive statements in nonassertive and assertive postures. (They need not move each other's bodies in this case.)

Important Note: Some people are uncomfortable about touching other people due to cultural or personality preferences. As always, give your learners the option not to participate in this game if it makes them uncomfortable. They will learn as much from watching and listening to the debriefing as from taking part.

OTHER TOPICS THIS GAME TEACHES

- Conflict and Negotiation
- Communication Skills

GAME 2—STUCK IN THE MIDDLE WITH YOU

THE POINT OF THIS GAME

Assertive people accurately **distinguish between the merits and potential consequences of their actions**. Often we decide to be assertive only after engaging in a spirited internal debate about it. This game lightheartedly illustrates the kind of inner dialogue we can (and should) go through when weighing the pros and cons of being assertive.

TIME NEEDED

10 minutes

MATERIALS NEEDED

Three prewritten placards large enough to be read across the room. One reads: A Nice, Normal Person Who Sometimes Hears Voices; another reads: Do it!; and the third reads: Don't Do It!

A Nice Normal Person Who Sometimes Hears Voices	Do It!	Don't Do It!

A SUGGESTED FUNNY INTRODUCTION

"Has anyone ever had a really good argument—with *yourself*? [Show of hands.] Have you ever actually come to *blows* with yourself? [Ask for another show of hands, this time looking slightly concerned.] Just checking. If you'd said yes, I'd have had to refer you to the company psychiatrist. Well, now, one of you in this room is going to have a good debate with yourself. And this time, *we* get to hear the voices inside your head! So without any further ado ... who wants to be the psychopath?"

[Look for a volunteer. Note: If no one raises a hand, use the volunteer-finding system described in Game 1.]

"You? Thank you! Come on down! And who wants to be the voices? You? And you? Thank you."

HOW TO PLAY THIS GAME

1. Have your learners brainstorm a list of reasons (or excuses) people might have for *not* acting assertively. Possible examples could include: "People will get angry at you," "It's quicker or easier to give in," or "Who are you to rock the boat?," Write these reasons on a whiteboard or flip chart paper.

2. Now brainstorm a list of reasons why someone *would* choose assertive action. (Examples: "You might actually get what you want," "You might get more respect," or "You might inspire others to speak up when they need to, reducing the amount of general passive-aggression around here.")

3. Have your learners come up with a situation in which a person might find it difficult to be assertive.

4. Your three volunteers now sit side by side, facing the rest of the group. The "psychopath" sits in the middle. (*Note:* This person will actually play someone legitimately deciding whether or not to be assertive in the situation the group described, so now is the time to say: "You're not *really* a psychopath in this game, so I'm going to stop using that word. Here. ..." Give the person the placard entitled "A Nice, Normal Person Who Hears Voices," and have the person hold it up for all to see. This will get a very respectable laugh.)

5. Now give the volunteer on the right the placard labeled Do It! This person will be the voice advising assertiveness. Give the one on the left the placard labeled Don't Do It! That person will be the voice advising *either* passive *or* aggressive behaviors.

6. Do It and Don't Do It now begin. Using the reasons the class brainstormed, they audibly whisper their arguments into the ears of the person in the middle, trying to convince that person to choose their side. (*Note:* If at any time they run out of reasons, they can ask for more suggestions from the rest of the group.)

7. After 5 minutes, stop the debate and ask the person in the middle to make a decision. Give all three volunteers a round of applause and have them return to their seats.

DEBRIEFING QUESTIONS

- How similar were the arguments you heard here to your own thought processes?
- Which arguments were more rational, and which ones more emotional?
- Were there any emotional arguments dressed up as rational ones?
- Have you ever had any thoughts or fears not expressed by our volunteers?
- What were the most compelling arguments the volunteers presented?
- What insights did you have about assertiveness? About fear? If *you* were the person stuck in the middle, would you have made the same decision? Why or why not?
- How will you change your next internal conversation about assertiveness? What arguments could you use on yourself that would be particularly effective?

TIPS ON MAKING THIS GAME WORK WELL

Remember that while Do It can only suggest assertiveness (i.e., stating one's own needs while remaining respectful of others'), Don't Do It can suggest either passive *or* aggressive behaviors. For example, that person can say, "Don't speak up. You want to

262

be seen as a whiner?" Conversely, the person can say, "Tell them where to get off! It's time someone laid down the law to those creeps!"

OTHER TOPICS THIS GAME TEACHES

Emotional Intelligence

GAME 3—ANIMAL KINGDOM

THE POINT OF THIS GAME

Assertive people are **aware of their own styles** in dealing with conflict. The humor in this game makes it easier for your learners to assess their own strengths and weaknesses in an honest way.

TIME NEEDED

10–20 minutes, depending on the size of the group

MATERIALS NEEDED

The following animal names should be posted around the room on separate pieces of paper: Gorilla, Ostrich, Snake, Skunk, Porcupine, Goldfish, Dove, Lion, Hyena, and Donkey. Also include a paper headed Other.

A SUGGESTED FUNNY INTRODUCTION

"Does anyone ever feel like you work in a zoo? Wait!! Don't answer that out loud! Just think about it. Sure, your colleagues may *look* like intelligent people when they walk into work, but once there, do they ever turn into snakes, skunks, and vultures? Is it really possible to work with, well, a bunch of *animals*?"

HOW TO PLAY THIS GAME

1. Have your learners look at the various animal types posted around the room, and describe how these animals typically

behave when they feel threatened. For example, an ostrich might hide its head in the sand until things are "safe," a gorilla might face down the enemy making impressive grunts and beating its chest menacingly, and so on.

2. Now ask your learners to think about their own style of responding to conflict. What's their first reaction in an argument with someone else? With all due respect to the animal kingdom, which of the animals posted would be most similar to them in behavior? (If no animal seems to fit, encourage the learners to also consider animals that are not posted in the room, or to imagine hybrid animals, like half lion and half donkey).

3. Direct everyone to stand under the animal that best represents themselves in conflict. (Again, they can stand under the Other posting if their animal isn't named or they see themselves as a hybrid.)

4. Go around the room and ask the learners to describe how they are similar to the animals they chose. (Example: "I'm like a skunk because I don't seek out conflicts, but when I'm in one I make sure I have the final and lasting word.")

DEBRIEFING QUESTIONS

- Were there any surprises in the animals you or someone else chose?

- What positive attributes does your animal have that you wish others recognized? What is generally misunderstood about your animal? What advice would you give someone else about working with your animal?

- What happens in the workplace when human "animals" of different species have conflicts? For example, what happens when the human equivalents of a snake and a donkey conflict?

- What happens when the same species of animals are angry with one another? For example, how might the human equivalent of two porcupines fight?

- **KEY POINT:** Based on the insights you've just gained about other people's styles, how might you work with your colleagues differently?

OTHER TOPICS THIS GAME TEACHES

- Communication Skills
- Emotional Intelligence
- Reducing Workplace Negativity
- Dealing with Difficult People

GAME 4—SHOOT-OUT AT THE O.K. CORRAL

THE POINT OF THIS GAME

Assertive people **define, communicate, and stick to their personal boundaries**. By setting limits and respectfully asking others to abide by them, assertive people live by their values. This game teaches a four-level boundary-setting model, and gives practice in communicating personal limits to others. Note that much of the laughter in this game is *nervous* laughter. This is not a bad thing; it has been found that a little negative emotion can, in fact, enhance learning. The debriefing begins in Round 2, specifically to allow you to help your learners grapple with their emotions as they go through the anxiety-producing process of insisting on their limits. Remember: This is a process that defeats many people! It is worth going through a little discomfort to master it.

TIME NEEDED

20–25 minutes

MATERIALS NEEDED

The Four-Level Assertiveness Model (see handout) photocopied or on a flip chart or overhead

A SUGGESTED FUNNY INTRODUCTION

"Anyone here ever work with a touchy-feelie type? You know the kind I mean: They stand too close. They pat you on the back, maybe even *hug* you! [Shudder.] They chat about their personal lives, ask you about yours. ... They're just too darned *friendly!* [Show of hands; nervous or venting laughter.]

"Good. Now how many have ever worked with a real *cold fish?* You know: the kind of person who doesn't *know* how to smile, talks incessantly about facts, figures, and quality control. ... They just have ice water in their veins! [Show of hands; more, perhaps retaliatory, laughter.] Great.

"We've just seen that different people have different boundaries—personal limits of behavior with which they themselves are comfortable.

"Now, how many here know that *your* boundaries are the *right* ones, and anything different is *bad?* [Show of hands. *Note:* you will usually get some humorous hand-raising, as attendees acknowledge that this is often their true feeling, and also that it is foolish. Be sure to acknowledge this healthy humor on their part! Make approving eye contact with one of the hand-raisers and say:] Of *course* you do! And you're right! If there's *anything* we humans agree on it's that 'My way is ... [Pause, and let them fill this in, which we guarantee they will:] the right way!' Yeah!

"Okay, so different people have different personal needs. Agreed? [Many learners will nod.] And often as not, this is not a *moral* issue, it's just personal taste. *Agreed?* [Nod.] But too often we *make* it a moral issue. Because we feel that our way is the right way, so naturally anyone else's must be wrong. And what this leads to is unassertive behavior on our part. For example, we don't simply say, 'Hey, I'd *prefer* it if you didn't stand so close. Would you mind humoring me on this?' Instead, we say something aggressive, like, 'Yo, back off, jerk!' Or else we passively skulk off and tell someone else what a rude creep this person is. Is this really fair?"

[*Note:* At this point, some of your learners will probably want to argue that it sometimes *is* fair, since some people really are out of line in this or that behavior, others won't listen to reason, and so on. Acknowledge the validity of their feelings. Then say:]

"Hold onto that thought. The exercise we're about to do will show you how to recognize the difference between behaviors you feel *personally uncomfortable about,* and those you really can't live with. It will also give you practice in communicating both things to another person, and in a way that is most likely to get you what you need. How many would like to know how to do this? [Show of hands. *Note:* Most people would love to know!] Well, if you're going to beg … *let's try it out!* Everybody stand up, please!"

HOW TO PLAY THIS GAME

ROUND 1:

1. Pair up your learners and ask them to stand facing each other about five feet apart.

2. Have the pairs move toward one another, one small step at a time, until one person in the pair starts to feel they're close enough. This will be Person A for the rest of the game. Person A now says: "This is as far as I want to go" and stops moving. Person B must likewise stop.

3. When all pairs have stopped, firmly instruct Persons B to *continue moving forward,* one tiny step at a time, until they have reached their own limit of comfort. (*Note:* This will create uncomfortable laughter, which is okay. Tell your learners that sometimes exploration *is* uncomfortable, and ask them to have faith and bear with you for just a few moments more.)

4. When all Persons B have stopped moving forward, say: "I now have a roomful of pairs with at least *one* partner who is uncomfortable. Am I right?" [This will get another laugh. Continue:]

5. "In fact, now *both* partners are probably somewhat uneasy, since Persons B know *for sure* that they just trespassed on Person A's comfort zone. No one really enjoys knowing this. For the moment, I'm going to relieve you all of your pain … *but you will come back to it.* [Another laugh, usually.] Persons

B, please give your partners a friendly 'I'm sorry,' and everybody return to your seats."

6. Give a 10-minute lecture on the four-Level Assertiveness Model.

ROUND 2:

1. Have the pairs reconvene into the exact formations they just left (i.e., comfortably spaced for one, but too close for the other).

2. Tell Persons A (the ones who set the first boundaries) to go to Level 1 of the Assertiveness Model. In whatever words they choose, they should politely ask their partners to step back a little. Example: "Excuse me, but would you mind if we stood a little farther apart? I have a problem standing so close to people. It distracts me."

3. Say: "Persons A, did you ask for what you need in the most polite and assertive way possible?" Wait for their acknowledgment of this. Then say: "Good! Persons B, smile at your partners and *stay where you are*!" (This will get a laugh, as the B's do just that, with varying degrees of discomfort.)

4. Say: "Persons A, how many of you are feeling a little *irritated* with your partners right now? [Show of hands; venting laughter.] If you are, then you need to move to Level 2—sticking to your boundaries. Politely repeat your previous request for your partner to move back, and remain respectful and firm." (Example: "Pardon me again. I really *do* need a little more space.")

5. Let Persons A do this. Then tell Persons B to cheerfully acknowledge this request and remain exactly where they are.

6. Say: "Persons A, how many of you feel like saying something rather nasty to your partners right now? [Show of hands, usually with *lots* of venting laughter from both A's and B's.] Okay, this is when most people usually back down: warning others about the consequences of not respecting their needs. We'll talk about choosing your fights later; for now, let's assume you *do* choose to insist on this boundary. What

is a consequence you could offer your partners if they *don't* comply with your needs?"

7. Work with the A's to differentiate consequences that are *assertive* (Example: walking away) from those that are *passive* (Example: continually moving backward) or *aggressive* (Examples: threatening or pushing your partner).

8. Ask Persons A to choose an assertive consequence, and state it to their partners. Then allow Persons B to decide whether or not to honor the request. If Persons A's needs are not met, they must then act upon whatever consequence they offered.

9. Tell all pairs: "Please shake hands, beg forgiveness, and sit down. Thank you."

DEBRIEFING QUESTIONS

- How hard or easy was it to be Person A and set the limits?
- What was it like to be Person B and ignore the requests?
- What are some reasons someone might ignore even an *assertive* request?
- What thoughts and emotions do we have when other people don't comply with our requests? How do these thoughts and feelings help us to find or prevent us from finding a win–win solution?
- Did any of the A's find they were willing to compromise on how far apart they stood from their partners? Did you see a difference between what you *don't like* and what you *can't live with*?
- **KEY POINTS:** How many regularly use *all four steps* when setting your limits? Has anyone used Step 1 and then backed off? Has anyone ever ignored Steps 1 to 3, and just exploded into Step 4: *"Die, vermin"*? Was that fair? What steps do you, personally, need to focus on in order to get your needs met?

TIPS ON MAKING THIS GAME WORK WELL

This game has the greatest impact when you pair up participants who differ from each other personally, culturally, and ethnically. A good way to make this happen is to start with an icebreaker in which learners reveal facts about themselves that are not immediately apparent.

OTHER TOPICS THIS GAME TEACHES

- Communication Skills
- Emotional Intelligence
- Dealing with Difficult People

THE FOUR-LEVEL ASSERTIVENESS MODEL

LEVEL 1: Set your personal limits by politely making your request. *Note: This is not a statement of your moral superiority!* It's just a simple, honest expression of your needs or wants. To keep it respectful, use the *"I"* statement: "Would you mind (stopping) _____? *I feel* °"

LEVEL 2: Politely reiterate your limits or boundaries. Remember that this is not *The Jerry Springer Show*. You *can* insist on your needs without punching someone out! In fact, you can even do it without being insulting. Consider saying, "Pardon me again. I really *do* need _____." (Tip: The fact that you haven't backed down after your first request will give this second request, mild-mannered though it is, a *lot* of power!)

LEVEL 3: Describe the consequences of not respecting your limits: "This is something that's important to me. If you can't _____, I'll have to _____." Note that your consequence may be as simple as walking away. Or it may be more painful. But be warned: *This is the point when most people back down, even when their needs are vital to their well-being or peace of mind!* Most of us are plain terrified of getting tough. Yet it is a fact of life that we must sometimes take action to protect our limits. (At the same time, remember that truly assertive people do *not* make physical threats—that's *Jerry Springer* again.)

LEVEL 4: Enforce the consequences: "I see you have chose not to comply. As promised, this means I will _____."

GAME 5—BIZARRO EXPERT

THE POINT OF THIS GAME

Assertive people **communicate difficult messages in ways that are less likely to put others on the defensive.** This game teaches a five-step model for confronting others, and reinforces the importance of using language that is respectful and specific. It also offers a unique strategy for harmlessly venting hostility. The game is constructed to enhance long-term retention of the material because of the way it gets your learners to turn the information upside-down, so to speak. Finally, it's a *great* game for sharing the spotlight!

TIME NEEDED

40–50 minutes, depending on the size of the group

MATERIALS NEEDED

- The 5-Step Confrontation Model (see handout), posted on a whiteboard or distributed as photocopies.
- Five pieces of flip chart paper and a minimum of five markers

A SUGGESTED FUNNY INTRODUCTION

[A good way to get people interested in any topic is to relate it to something they have strong feelings about. In our experience, many people feel *very* strongly about this:]

"Anybody ever have the experience of working with someone who just doesn't seem to like you? Perhaps this person ignores you, or even worse, finds ways to insult you and your ideas in front of other people. It's not something you can just ignore, is it? Nope! So, even if you hate confrontation, this is one of those times when you have no choice.

"Now, as with so many challenges, it's not what you do, but how you do it. Living inside most of us are at least two opposing 'experts' who give us advice. One side is Dr. Bizarro. Dr. Bizarro advises you on elaborate revenge fantasies, and is the expert whose voice reigns supreme when you're muttering to yourself at 2 a.m. Here's what Dr. Bizarro would advise you to say:

[Arrange yourself in front of a learner, using nice, assertive posture. Look at the person with a friendly expression and say, in a pleasant tone:] 'Mr. or Ms. Brown, I'd like to ask you a question in all sincerity. What the flaming heck is your problem? Were you dropped a lot as an infant, perhaps? You clearly don't relate to your own species. I suggest you see a therapist. To motivate you in that direction, I will be happy to make you suffer for everything you have put me and the rest of humankind through. From now on, Mr. or Ms. Brown, the name of the game is watch your back. Have I made myself clear? Good. I'm glad we had this little talk.'

"How many of you have heard Dr. Bizarro's voice in your head, giving you this sort of advice?

"Assuming you don't actually take Dr. Bizarro's advice and say these things in real life, what might be the positive benefits of this sort of venting? [Possible responses: releases your anger, improves your sense of power, taps into your humor.]

"What does Dr. Bizarro really want from this conversation?" [Possible responses: make the other person feel intimidated, take revenge, make self feel better through insults and threats.]

"What would most likely happen next if you did take Dr. Bizarro's advice and actually confronted a colleague or boss like this? What would the other person most likely feel and do? [Possible responses: feel defensive and then attack, back down in public but continue to sabotage you in private, back down completely, or escalate the behavior.]

"What's the likelihood that you would gain a better understanding with the other person if you followed Dr. Bizarro's advice?" [Answer: slim to none.]

"There is another expert living inside your head, whose voice perhaps isn't as loud or interesting as Dr. Bizarro's but who can suggest a method with a better probability for success. This is Dr. Judicious, who will suggest a five-step model for handling confrontation."

HOW TO PLAY THIS GAME

1. Describe the model using flip chart paper or handouts.

   Step 1: Describe not the negative present, but the positive future you hope for as a result of the confrontation. In this case, you might say something like, "I'd like us to have a better relationship and feel more comfortable working together."

   Step 2: Describe the problem *specifically*. Let's say you feel that your colleague disparages you in front of other people. You could say something like: "Three times in our last group meeting, you rolled your eyes when I spoke, and you described my idea about the conversion as naive."

   Step 3: State why this behavior is problem, on the assumption that the person really doesn't know. You would add to your statement and say: "When you do this, I feel insulted and belittled. We seem to spend too much of our energy fighting each other instead of working on the project."

   Step 4: Offer a solution: "When you disagree with my ideas, I'd like you tell me so in a respectful manner so that I can hear your objections fairly. I would like you to use more respectful body language and to evaluate my ideas carefully before labeling them as naive or wrong."

   Step 5: End on a positive note. "If you can do that, I think I'll be in a better position to help support your goals and ideas."

2. Ask for someone in the group to describe an experience they've had in which direct confrontation was needed (i.e., when other, subtler forms of assertiveness did not work).

3. Divide the group into teams of 5 to 7, give each team a piece of flip chart paper and markers, and assign each team to one of the steps in the model. Using the situation just described, ask the teams to come up with as many statements as they can that match their step. But before they begin, say:

4. "You remember the first confrontation I demonstrated with Dr. Bizarro? Dr. Bizarro is well aware of Dr. Judicious' five-step model, but he has corrupted the meanings to suit his own perverse ideas. Dr. Bizarro has written a book outlining these five steps, but with totally opposite meanings. For example, he interpreted Step 1, Describe the positive future, to mean you say something like, 'I can't wait till you get out of my face.' Step 2, 'State the problem specifically, meant 'You are a ****** and that's why we have this problem!' As you brainstorm your statements, I want you to also include some from Dr. Bizarro's book. Any questions? Go!"

5. Give the teams 10 minutes to develop their lists. Ask them to put the letter B beside any Bizarro statements.

6. Ask the teams to choose their best Dr. Bizarro and Dr. Judicious statements.

7. Ask for one representative from each group to stand in the front of the room in numerical order. One by one, have the teams present their Dr. Judicious statements to the entire group. The statements should flow together to form a coherent message that illustrates the model.

8. Next, ask the representatives to share their Dr. Bizarro statements with the group so that they also form a coherent message demonstrating Dr. B's model. As always, lead the laughter when they read their humorous contributions.

9. If there is time, post the flip chart papers with the remaining statements and ask each group to read its statements aloud.

DEBRIEFING QUESTIONS

- How hard or easy was it to generate statements for your step of the model? What criteria did you use to judge your best statement?

- What might be the benefits of using a confrontation script before facing down a difficult person? What could you do to give yourself time to come up with a script when you are in the heat of anger?

- How might you use this model in real life?

- How did it feel to write the Dr. Bizarro statements? Was there an element of enjoyment to be able to vent so dramatically? [*Tip:* Now's a good time to repeat one or two of them. They will get laughs all over again, and the learners who wrote them will positively glow.]

- We do need to vent. But when we vent to the person we're angry at, what's generally the result? Do you think it could be useful to vent by writing Dr. Bizarro lines into your confrontation script, and then not use them?

- Considering what we've learned from this activity, how will you change your approach in your next difficult conversation?

OTHER TOPICS THIS GAME TEACHES

- Dealing with Difficult People
- Reducing Workplace Negativity

The 5-Step Confrontation Model

√ Step 1: Describe the Positive Future

√ Step 2: Describe the Problem Specifically

√ Step 3: State Why This Is a Problem

√ Step 4: Offer a Positive Solution

√ Step 5: End on a Positive Note

ABOUT THE AUTHORS

Doni Tamblyn is President of the San Francisco–based training company, Humor Rules. Over the past 10 years she has delivered hundreds of seminars and presentations to organizations around the world.

Sharyn Weiss is a performance consultant and trainer with 15 years of experience working with nonprofit and corporate groups. She has an MA in Training and Development. This is her second book on experiential training.